CHRONICLE

OF THE

GREY FRIARS OF LONDON.

EDITED BY

JOHN GOUGH NICHOLS,

F.S.A. LOND. AND NEWC.

PRINTED FOR THE CAMDEN SOCIETY.

M.DCCC.LII.

Reprinted with the permission of the Royal Historical Society

AMS PRESS

NEW YORK • LONDON

First AMS EDITION published 1968
Manufactured in the United States of America

Series No. I, 53

AMS PRESS, INC.
NEW YORK, N.Y. 10003

PREFACE.

THE present Chronicle has hitherto remained not merely unpublished, but almost wholly unnoticed. It is now presented to the Camden Society in a full conviction of its value.

The Editor has given it the title of THE CHRONICLE OF THE GREY FRIARS OF LONDON: to which it has an indisputable claim, inasmuch as it formed a portion of the Register-book of that fraternity. This title, however, must be taken merely as distinguishing the present compilation from others of the same class, and not as explanatory of its contents. In its original character it is not a religious but a civic Chronicle.

It is well known that history, in the form of Chronicles, was a favourite portion of the literature of the middle ages. The annals of a country were usually kept according to the years of the sovereign's power, and not those of the Christian æra. The Chronicles compiled in large cities were arranged in like manner, with the years reckoned according to the annual succession of chief magistrates. Thus, in the present instance, though the Chronicle is primarily arranged in reigns, and the years are numbered by those reigns, yet the period of time included in each year commences with the London mayoralty at the end of October, and the events which follow belong not only to the two ensuing months of that year of our Lord, but also to the next year until the end of October; and not only to that year of the king's reign, but to a portion more or less of the next year of the reign, according as the date of the accession of the monarch varied from that of the Mayor's entrance into office.[a]

The present compilation is therefore properly a London Chronicle; but the Editor deemed it unnecessary to copy from the manuscript the succession it contains of Mayors and Sheriffs, as their names have now been frequently printed elsewhere in other London Chronicles, and in fact in its earlier portions the manuscript consists of little else. Nor would the book have been worth printing at all in its original character of a London Chronicle, had it been nothing more; for in the early reigns its entries are slight and fragmentary, and occasionally incorrect, as some of the marginal notes will show.

It was usual for London Chronicles to commence with the reign of Richard the First, that being the date from which the roll of chief magistrates, at first termed Bailiffs, had been preserved. Such is the case with a Latin Chronicle kept in the Town Clerk's office, and which has been already presented to the Camden Society under the title of "Liber de Antiquis Legibus." Its narrative descends only to the year 1274. The French Chronicle of London, which has also been printed for the Camden Society, embraces the period from 1259 to 1343. The English Chronicle of London, which was edited by Sir Harris Nicolas, commences with the civic æra of 1189, the 1st Richard I. and extends to the year 1483. Some portions of it are highly curious. Arnold's Chronicle, like our own,

[a] Appended to Grafton's Chronicle will be found a table constructed for the express purpose of meeting the difficulties which arose from the mode of reckoning above described. It is entitled "A Table declaring the reignes of everie King of this realme sithen the conquest, and the yeares of our Lorde and monethes and dayes of their beginning, and also the names and surnames of all the Maiors and Shirifes of London, with the yere and daye of their entrance into their charge." For every year this table presents four dates: 1. the commencement of the year of our Lord, which was the 25th March; 2. that of the King's accession, as the case might be; 3. that of the entrance into office of the Bailiffs and Sheriffs, which was the 28th September; and 4. that of the entrance into office of the Mayor, the 28th October. It extends from A.D. 1189 to 1568.

is little more than a list of Mayors and Sheriffs: it commences at the same period, and extends to 1520. Two other London Chronicles still in manuscript are described in the annexed note.[a] Besides these, Fabyan's printed Chronicle is to be classed as a London one. His name concludes the list; for though Grafton, Holinshed, and the indefatigable John Stowe, and others beside, may have been Londoners, their books were general Chronicles, and not arranged according to the succession of Mayors and Sheriffs.

Of all the foregoing, Arnold's Chronicle is that which most nearly resembles the present, detailing the same events, though not quite

[a] The following List of London Chronicles may be found useful:

1. [In Latin.] Liber de Antiquis Legibus: extending from 1189 to 1274. Printed for the Camden Society, 1846.

2. [In French.] The French Chronicle of London: from 1259 to 1343. Printed for the Camden Society, 1844.

3. [In Latin.] The MS. Harl. 5444: from 1195 to 1316.

4. [In English.] The MS. Arundel XIX. in the College of Arms: from 1189 to 1451. It is prepared in blank to last to 1475, and there are some additions, but of little importance, down to 1522. (See the preface to the French Chronicle of London, p. ii.)

5. [In English.] The Chronicle of London, edited by Sir Harris Nicolas, in 4to. 1827, from the MS. Harl. 565, and MS. Cotton. Julius, B. I. extending from 1188 to 1483.—Another MS., but with considerable variations, which was unknown to Sir Harris Nicolas, is preserved in the MS. Cotton. Cleopatra, C. iv. ff. 21—61. It commences with the expedition to Harfleur in 1415, and terminates, like the MS. Harl. 565, in 1443.

6. A Tablet which hung at the tomb of the Duke of Lancaster in St. Paul's cathedral, contained a brief chronicle in Latin and English. See this printed in the same volume, pp. 174—187, and from the same MS. It extends to the coronation of Henry VI. at Paris in 1432.

7. Arnold's Chronicle: from 1189 to 1520. The greater part of this book consists of charters, bulls, ordinances, and formularies for legal documents. It was reprinted, under the editorship of Dr. Dibdin, in 4to. 1811, with this title: "The Customs of London, otherwise called Arnold's Chronicle; containing, among divers other matters, the original of the celebrated Poem of The Nut-Brown Maid. Reprinted from the First Edition, with the additions included in the Second."

8. Fabyan's Chronicle: from the earliest times to the year 1516; and continued in subsequent editions to 1533, to 1542, and to 1559. Reprinted in 1811, 4to. edited by Sir Henry Ellis.

so fully, down to the 17th Hen. VII. A.D. 1502. After that date, these two London Chronicles are wholly different in their contents.

Stowe had either the possession or the loan of the manuscript before us, and his small and compact hand is to be seen in two or three places in correction of the original writer.[a] But we do not find that he made full use of it: of its passages relative to religious matters, which are the most curious of the whole, he has given but a small portion; and our Chronicle escaped the research of the equally industrious, and still more voluminous, ecclesiastical historian, the Rev. John Strype.

It is towards the end of the reign of Henry the Eighth that this Chronicle begins to have a character of its own. The writer had a watchful regard to the religious changes of the times, and he naturally recorded those in particular which occurred within the sphere of his personal observation, in the city of London, and in the metropolitan church of St. Paul. He appears to have retained possession of the book after the dissolution of the house of Grey Friars, and the dismissal of the rest of his fraternity; and from that time we may suppose that he continued his record in pursuance of his old habits, with no other object than his own satisfaction. It is therefore not to the Grey Friars as a body, or to the attention and accuracy of their successive registrars, that we have to attribute the chief historical value that exists in the following pages; but rather to the individual merit of him whom we may fairly regard as the last of the

[a] Stowe has written the word "falce" against the passage stating the poisoning of king John in fol. 337 b. At the foot of fol. 343 is written in Stowe's hand:—

"John Brian shrive [see p. 14 of the present volume] was drownyd by seint Katheryns mylle. Reg. 6."

Another of his corrections is described in the note at p. 15.

He names the "Reg. of the Gray Fryers" as his authority for the story of lady Hungerford. (Chronicle, edit. 1631, p. 517.)

London Franciscans. Beyond these circumstances, we have no evidence upon which any speculations can be founded as to his name or position. From his frequent notices of Saint Paul's it might be surmised that he had some official connection with the cathedral church; but the close vicinity of his residence would alone afford him sufficient opportunities of observation.

With these brief remarks our Chronicle may be left to the just appreciation of the reader. Some notice, however, is due to the Fraternity in whose Register it was recorded. Though the Chronicle itself contains but few and incidental items of their history, they were by no means negligent of its due commemoration: but that was done in another shape, and in the Latin language, in an earlier part of the same volume. This Register is, in fact, one of the amplest authorities for the history of the Friars Minors, as they once flourished in England; and a descriptive account of the whole volume cannot be deemed inappropriate in this place.

It may be acceptable to prefix a few historical dates, derived in part from the same source. Saint Francis, the founder and patron of the Friars Minors,[a] was born at Assisi in Italy in the year 1182; and he was still a young man when he commenced his scheme of religious observance. The Rule of his Fraternity was approved by Pope Innocent III. in 1210, revised in the Lateran council of 1215, and confirmed by Honorius III. in 1224. At the first general convention of the fraternity in 1217 its numbers were already considerable; and in 1219 it consisted of more than five thousand members. Elate with his success, Francis determined to appoint Provincial

[a] This designation was adopted in token of their deep humility: Fuller supposed in allusion to Jacob's words in Gen. xxxii. 10, *Sum* Minor *omnibus beneficiis tuis.*—Church Hist. vi. 270.

Ministers in the principal kingdoms of Europe. In the year 1224, two years before the death of their founder,[a] a deputation of nine of the fraternity, four clerics and five laics, arrived in England, with letters recommendatory from Pope Honorius III. and took up their first residence in the Benedictine priory of the Holy Trinity at Canterbury, in which city five of their number soon after formed the first Franciscan convent in England.

The other four proceeded to London, and were first entertained for fifteen days in the house of the Friars Preachers, or Dominicans. Afterwards they hired a house in Cornhill of John Travers, then sheriff, where they made some small cells, and continued until the following summer, when the devotion of the citizens enabled them to remove to the site of their future residence near Newgate. Their first and principal benefactor was John Iwyn, citizen and mercer, who gave them some land and houses in the parish of St. Nicholas in the Shambles, by deed dated in the 9th Hen. III. Upon this they erected their original building. The first chapel, which became the choir of the church, was built at the cost of sir William Joyner, who was mayor of London in 1239; the nave was added by sir Henry Waleys, who was mayor during several years of the reign of Edward I.;[b] the chapter-house by Walter the potter, citizen and

[a] Among the other numerous errors of Mr. Stevens in his Supplementary Monasticon (adverted to hereafter) is a misprint, p. 112, of "1224" for 1226, as the date of the death of Saint Francis.

[b] After Walter Hervy, who was mayor of London at the accession of Edward I., there were only three mayors during the thirty-five years of his reign. Walter Hervy had been elected by the citizens in the last year of Henry III. (see the French Chronicle of London, p. 11), but for some time after the chief magistrate was elected by the aldermen only, and the office became in consequence almost perpetual. Henry Waleys was Hervy's successor for one year; then Gregory de Rokesley (presently mentioned in the text) for seven years; and then Waleys for four years; after which the king seized the liberties of the city into his own hands, and appointed a *custos* or warden, who continued for twelve years.

alderman (sheriff in 1270 and 1273), who also presented all the brazen pots necessary for the kitchen, infirmary, and other offices; the dormitory was erected by sir Gregory de Rokesley,[a] mayor from 1275 to 1282; the refectory by Bartholomew de Castro, another citizen; the infirmary by Peter de Helyland; and the studies by Bonde, king of the heralds.

The principal contributor to the cost of supplying the convent with water was William, called from his trade the Taylor, and who served King Henry the Third in that capacity.[b]

Waleys was then reappointed, and died mayor in 1302; after which Sir John le Blount was mayor during the six remaining years of Edward's reign. It is very possible that Waleys and Rokesley had the credit of erecting the buildings of the Grey Friars, not because they were done at their personal expense, but by contributions of the citizens under their patronage and superintendence. Waleys was apparently an equal or greater benefactor to the house of Franciscan Sisters without Aldgate, in whose chapel his bones were laid to rest. See the note upon him in the French Chronicle of London, p. 12.

[a] Rokesley was buried in the church of the Grey Friars; but a perpetual chantry for the repose of his soul was established in the church of St. Mary Woolnoth. See the note, ibid. p. 20.

[b] The chapter of the Register from which these particulars are abstracted may be transcribed as a specimen of this very curious record:—

Prima fundacio ecclesiæ Fratrum Minorum London.

In primis CAPELLAM, quæ postmodum facta est magna pars Chori, construxit eis dominus Willielmus Joyner, et ad alias domos construendas donavit per vices expensas .cc. libras sterlingorum.

NAVEM ecclesiæ construxit magnis sumptibus dominus Henricus de Galis [*i. e.* Waleys], maior London. et per multos annos redditus quos fratres solvebant diversis domibus aliorum religiosorum redemit, et fratres de illis redditibus deoneravit; cujus memoria in benedictione sit eterna. Amen.

CAPITULUM eis construxit dominus Walterus le potter, civis et aldermanus London. et omnia vasa erea pro coquina, infirmaria, et aliis officinis necessaria eciam donavit.

VESTIBULUM constructum est de bonis communibus. [*This was a slip of the writer's pen, for it was against the rule of his order to claim any property whatever, so he added,* elimosinis scilicet, *and made this insertion,* Frater Thomas Feltham istud elongavit et multipliciter adornavit armariis tam inferius quam superius. Et aquaductum de pissina communis lavatorii illud [*l.* illuc] adduxit, [et] multa utilia a[lia] procuravit. *Stevens has mistranslated this,* "and brought thither the Aqueduct of most pure Water for the com-

A more magnificent church was erected about a century later, when first the choir was rebuilt, chiefly at the cost of Margaret of France, the second wife of king Edward the First, who assigned it for her place of interment; and the nave was added from the bene-

mon Washing," *instead of,* "And he brought thither a water-pipe from the cistern of the Common Lavatory," *which was in the Cloister, as is stated more precisely afterwards. In the letters patent of* 38 *Hen. VIII. it is described as* "unum lavacrum cupri duplicatum cum plumbo continentem per estimationem in longitudine octodecim acras et in profunditate duos pedes et dimidium."

Dormitorium totum cum lectis et cameris necessariis construxit dominus Gregorius de Rokysley maior Londinensis.

Refectorium construxit dominus Bartholomeus de Castro civis Londinensis, et pavit semper fratres in die sancti Bartholomei.

Altaria vero quæ se extendunt in longum versus austrum constructa fuerunt de diversis communibus elimosinis. Sed dominus Henricus de Galeys dedit meremeum, cujus memoria in benedictione sit. Amen. *Stevens apparently misreád* meremeum (*the timber*) *as* incrementum, *for he has translated it* "the Improvement."

Infirmariam construxit pro magna parte Petrus de Helyland, dando ad ejus constructionem .c. libras sterlingorum.

Studia pro magna parte constructa fuerunt de bonis Bonde Regis heraldorum. Le roi de heraus. *Stevens misread the latter words* Henry Heruns. *The party is a king of the heralds not mentioned in Noble's History of the College of Arms. Stowe calls him* Bevis Bond, *I suspect from misreading the words* bonis Bonde, *which are both in red ink, like other proper names in the MS. Mr. Trollope (p.* 8*) has altered* Bevis *to* Roger, *I do not know whether on any authority.*

Aqueductum construxerunt infra scripti. In primis caput aqueductus contulit Willielmus Taylour, sartor domini Henrici regis tercii post conquestum, ad instanciam fratris Willielmi de Basynges, qui totum aqueductum procuravit et usque ad finem complevit. Set expensas sive sumptus administraverunt felicis recordationis dominus Henricus rex Angliæ illustris supramemoratus, Salekynus de Basynge optimæ indolis adolescens, dominus Henricus de Frowyke, et dominus Henricus de Basynges milites. Isti fuerunt cooperatores et coadjutores præcipui. Et postea frater Galfridus de Camera novam domum in secundo capite construxit et antiquam melioravit, et omnes defectus notabiles investigavit et correxit, et multa bona pro eodem procuravit et fecit; cujus adjutores præcipui fuerunt Alanus Gille cum consorte sua civis Lond', dominus Henricus Darcy qui dedit .c. solidos pro cistrina de bonis, Johannes Tryple eciam coadjuvantes opus compleverunt. Pro cujus eciam anima fratres minores habuerunt Londini omnibus computatis .c. et x li. et xvij s. v d. q[a]. Cujus animæ propicietur Deus. Amen. *Though these latter clauses are not very clear, it would seem that the rents, amounting to* 110*l.* 17*s.* 5¼*d. were wholly derived from the bene-*

factions of John of Britany, Earl of Richmond, and his niece Mary Countess of Pembroke. It was 300 feet long, 89 feet wide, and 64 feet high. All the columns and the pavement were of marble.[a] This church was completed in 1327, having been twenty-one years in building. It suffered considerable injury from a storm in the year 1343,[b] and was then restored by the king, from regard to the memory of his mother.

factions of John Tryple, or from his goods after death, for the true reading is very probably de bonis Johannis Tryple. *Stevens, however, has given a very different version:* "The Friars Minors had at London, all Things computed, 110*l.* 17*s.* 5¼*d.*, to whose Souls God be merciful, *Amen.*"

[Next follows, "Ut sciatur posicio canalium aqueductus fratrum Minorum Lond' "—a very curious description. The main channel or pipe is traced under Newgate, through the rivulet at Holborn-bridge, up Leather-lane ("Liwrone-lane"), and so to the conduit-heads in the fields. Having a vacant page, I have appended this to the Preface, at p. xxxiv.

Postmodum autem frater Thomas de Feltham de pissina communis lavacri in claustro lavatorium ad vestibulum advexit, et multa bona in vestibulo expendit anno domini M[l].cc. (*blank*). Item anno domini 1422° renovata sunt lavacra in claustro, cum deposito fratris Roberti Yongge. Summa expensarum 27 li. 9 s. 1 d. ob.

Dispensam Hospitum cum cameris versus Infirmariam procuravit frater Ricardus Knotte, et multa alia bona habuerunt fratres de procuratione ejus a Willielmo Albone.

Scolæ cum Locutorio dispensa, cum cameris, et alia edificia necessaria constructa sunt de bonis communibus sicut fieri poterant, quia parva erant omnia et non multum sumptuosa; et in hiis morabantur fratres usque ad annum domini 136°. Tempore vero prædicto multum crevit erga fratres et conventum devotio et affectio fidelium, et secundum eam consequenter crevit fratrum numerosa multitudo in tantum quod aliquando centum, aliquando plures, et raro pauciores conventuales fratres London' habebantur. Et loca constructa quæ pro paucis sufficiebant postea tam multis sufficere non poterant, et idcirco nova et ampliora fideles inceperunt ipsis construere prout inferius declaratur. &c. &c.

[a] *Descriptio longitudinis et latitudinis ecclesiæ et altitudinis supradictæ.* In primis continet ecclesia in longitudine ccc. pedum de pedibus Sancti Pauli. Item in latitudine iiij[xx]ix. pedum de pedibus Sancti Pauli. Item in altitudine a terra usque ad tectum lxiiij. pedum de pedibus Sancti Pauli. Et ut patet omnes columpnæ et [*l.* sunt] de marmore et totum pavimentum de marmore. (Register, fol. 325 b.) Malcolm says of the present Christ church that "the pavement is partially composed of coarse red marble, which is evidently part of that of the old church of the Grey Friars." Londinium Redivivum, iii. 345.

[b] A notice of this occurs in the French Chronicle of London, p. 87.

The library was a later addition to the house,[a] and owed its foundation to the liberality of Sir Richard Whittington, the celebrated mayor in the reign of Henry the Fifth.

The few particulars which our Chronicle contains of the history of the Grey Friars may here be briefly indicated. Their arrival in England is noted under the 7th Hen. III.;[b] and their first provincial chapter in London in the last year of Henry V.[c] In 1456 is recorded the activity of their provincial, doctor Goddard, in appeaching Peacock bishop of Chichester of heresy.[d] In August, 1498, was the second provincial chapter of the Friars Minors in London: the stricter order of the Observants commencing at the same time.[e] On Saint George's day, 1502, they relinquished the "London russet," which they had for some time worn, and resumed the undyed white-grey which had been their original habit.[f] On the feast of Saint Francis, July 16, 1508, the mayor and aldermen were

[a] *De fundacione librariæ.* Anno domini M°. cccc°. xxj°. venerabilis vir Ricardus Wyttyngton mercer et maior Lond' incepit novam librariam, posuitque primum lapidem fundalem xxj°. die Octobris, in festo sancti Hillarionis abbatis. Et anno sequente ante festum Nativitatis Christi fuit domus errata (erecta?) et cooperta. Et in tribus annis sequentibus fuit terrata (i.e. *floored*), dealbata, vitrata, ambonibus, scannis (*l.* scamnis) et cellatura ornata (i.e. *furnished with desks, settles, and wainscoting or ceiling; not, as Stevens makes it,* "shelves, statues, and carving.") Et libris instaurata. Et expensæ factæ circa prædicta se extendunt ad ccccc.lvj. li. 16 s. 8 d. de qua summa solvit prædictus Ricardus Whyttyngton cccc. li. et residuum solvit Reverendus pater frater Thomas Wynchelsey et amici sui: quorum animabus propicietur Deus. Amen. *Stowe has amplified this description of Whittington's Library by stating that it was* "129 foot in length and 31 in breadth, all wainscoted about, having twenty-eight desks, and eight double settles of wainscot." *The admeasurements were probably his own taking: the desks and double settles, and books on the desks, are enumerated in king Henry's letters patent.*

Item pro scripto doctoris De lira in 2^bus^ volu^bus^ jacente jam in cathenis c. marcas, de quibus frater Johannes Frensche remisit 20*s*.

Item pro 4^or^. archangelis circa sepulturam Reginæ Isabellæ, 37*s*.

Item pro lectura domini Hostiensis jam jacentis in cathenis, 5 marcas. (fol. 325, b.)

[b] P. 3. [c] P. 15. [d] P. 20. [e] P. 26.

[f] Compare the three several statements in pp. 27, 28, and the note.

received with procession as founders, a custom which continued long after;[a] but it was not until 1522 that the convent began to provide a feast for the corporation on that anniversary.[b] In 1524 king Henry and cardinal Wolsey personally visited the house; and shortly after William Renscrofte, a refractory lay brother of the Observants of Greenwich, was committed to the custody of the Franciscans.[c] The next year they were visited by doctor Alleyn on the part of the cardinal.[d] In 1528, in the case of a prisoner who had broken away from the sessions at Newgate,[e] the convent asserted its right of sanctuary, a privilege that could scarcely be often put in requisition, as the much-frequented sanctuary of Saint Martin le Grand was in the immediate vicinity.

The Friars Observants and the Carthusians[f] were strenuous in their opposition to the religious changes made by King Henry VIII. The Franciscans seem to have acquiesced in the course of events more passively, and the only part those in London are recorded to have taken was to give sepulture to some of the victims of the tyrant's displeasure. The corpse of the holy Maid of Kent was interred in their cemetery,[g] as were several of the Northern rebels.[h] On the 12th Nov. 1539, Thomas Chapman, doctor of divinity, their warden, and twenty-five of his brethren, signed and sealed their deed of surrender to the King, which they professed to be the result of their having arrived at a profound conviction "that the perfeccion of Christian livyng dothe not consiste in dome ceremonyes, weryng of a grey coatte, disgeasing our selffes aftyr straunge fassions, dokynges, nodyngs, and bekynges, in gurdyng owr selffes wythe a gurdle full of knots, and other like papisticall ceremonyes, wherin

[a] P. 29. [b] P. 31. [c] Pp. 31, 32. [d] P. 33.
[e] P. 34. [f] See pp. 37, 38. [g] P. 37. [h] P. 41.

we have byn moost pryncipally practysed and misse-lyd in tymes past; but the very tru waye to please God, and to live a tru Christian man, wythe owte all ypocrasie and fayned dissimulacion, is sinceerly declaryd unto us by owre master Christe, his evangelists and apostoles:" wherefore they declared their determination thenceforth to "conform our selffes unto the will and pleasure of owr Supreme Hed undre God, in erthe, the King's Majestie, and not to follow the supersticious tradicions of ony foryncicall potentate or peere."

The terms of this surrender might be thought to have been dictated to the friars [a] by the King's ministers, were they not perfectly in accordance with a letter written by the warden to lord Cromwell, in which he begs for "a dispensation of our papistical slanderous apparel, the which I think it pleaseth God that we shall no more wear," [b] and "to change all customs, usages, and manners, the living and apparel that hath been offensive to God's people."

After the surrender, the house of the Grey Friars was not given up to immediate destruction. It appears to have remained unoccupied, in the King's hands, until the year 1544, when, together with the houses of the late Austin and Black Friars, it became a receptacle for the merchandise captured at sea from the French. We are told in our Chronicle [c] that every part of the Grey Friars' church was on this occasion filled with wine; but, except the injury it might sustain by such rough usage, it had not hitherto been

[a] It is, however, to be remarked that the surrenders of the Franciscans of Coventry and of Stamford contain precisely the same expressions; see Fuller's History of Abbeys, p. 319, Stevens's Monasticon, i. 139, 157, or the new Monasticon, vi. 1514, 1534. It may, therefore, be concluded that they were generally adopted through the fraternity.

[b] See this letter in Malcolm's Londinium Redivivum, vol. iii. p. 330; and, with the deed of surrender, in Trollope's History of Christ's Hospital.

[c] P. 48.

dismantled. King Henry's letters patent of 1546 shew that the "partitions" or screens remained both in the church and chancel, the altars, pictures, images, and pulpit; the monuments and gravestones; the candlesticks, organs, and desks.[a]

We have seen how the convent had been originally established by the charity of the principal citizens, how its library had been added by the bounty of Whittington, and how the mayor and aldermen were recognised as the "founders." Like other "founders," or patrons of religious houses, at this crisis, they would naturally be inclined to urge those hereditary claims which were advanced, with more or less success, by various proprietors who occupied a similar position throughout the country; and many Londoners, though perplexed by the new doctrines, and intimidated by the arbitrary measures of the sovereign, would retain some desire for the preservation of this magnificent church. In the latter days of King Henry, when he exhibited signs of returning sympathy with the interests of religion, he was induced to make an important grant to the city, for the general relief of the poor, and for the maintenance of divine service in the quarter where the Franciscans had flourished. It consisted of the whole church of the late Friars Minors, and the whole site of their house, the buildings called the Fratrye, the Lybrarie, the Dortor, and the Chapiter House; the Great Cloyster, and the Littell Cloyster; including all the chambers and buildings which had been recently in the tenures of George

[a] From an entry in the parish books of Christ Church seen by Malcolm it appears that, when the property was transferred to the city, there were 600 ounces of plate in the sacristy valued at 150*l.*, copes, vestments and other ornaments estimated at 200*l.*, the bells 100*l.*, the altars, chapels, stones, pews, iron, &c. 50*l.*, the church itself, the lead, timber, and soil thereof, 300*l.*—total 800*l.*; and the lands belonging to it were valued at 50*l.* 16*s.* per ann.—Lond. Red. iii. 334.

Woodward and Edward Metcalf, those which had been occupied by Owen Mone, the Hall and cellar beneath it occupied by Hugh Willoughby, one of the king's serjeants-at-arms, and other buildings on the north of the Little Cloister occupied by Richard Tredray; further, the king conveyed to the mayor, commonalty, and citizens by the same grant all the late hospital of Saint Bartholomew in West Smithfield, with the church thereof, several contiguous houses, and numerous small estates in all parts of the city which had belonged to the same hospital, as well as some in distant parts of the country; also the parish churches of Saint Nicholas and Saint Ewen within Newgate, with some adjacent tenements. It was arranged that the church of the Friars Minors should become a parish church, to be called by the name of Christ's church within Newgate, and be parochial for all the inhabitants within the two parishes of Saint Nicholas and Saint Ewen (which two churches it was intended to remove), and for that part of the parish of Saint Sepulchre which lay within Newgate, which gate was also to be reputed as being within the said parish. The church of the late hospital of Saint Bartholomew was in like manner to become a parish church, under the designation of Saint Bartholomew the Less. The mayor and citizens were to be the future patrons of both churches; but Thomas Birkehed was appointed the first vicar of Christ church by the king's letters patent, with a yearly pension of 26*l.* 13*s.* 4*d.* Further, the mayor and citizens were empowered to appoint one priest to be visitor of Newgate, with an annual stipend of 10*l.*; and five other priests in Christ church "in aid of the vicar in celebrating divine services and administering the sacraments and *sacramentalia* there," each of whom was to receive 8*l.* yearly; also one other priest in the late hospital, which was now to be called the House of the Poor in

West Smithfield, and who was to be designated the Hospitler. The hospital was to accommodate one hundred aged, sick, or impotent men and women, attended on by a matron, twelve nurses, and a resident surgeon. The corporation of London was bound to sustain these establishments by indentures made with the king, dated the 27th December, 1546, and the estates were granted and the foundation confirmed by letters patent dated on the 13th January following.[a]

Meanwhile, on the 3rd of January, being the first Sunday in the new year, as related in our Chronicle, the church that was sometime the Grey Friars' was again set open, and mass said at the altars—it will be recollected that no English service had hitherto been established—by divers priests.[b] On the same day, as Stowe tells us, doctor Ridley, then bishop of Rochester—and who, only a few months after, succeeded Bonner in the see of London—preached at Paul's Cross, declaring the king's gift, how that he had bestowed, for the relief of the poor, the hospital of Saint Bartholomew in Smithfield, lately valued at 305*l.* 6*s.* 7*d.*, and the church of the Grey Friars, valued at 32*l.* 19*s.* 7*d.*, and for the maintenance of the new parish church of Christ church had assigned lands valued at five hundred marks.

It was probably imagined that the pomp with which the new year witnessed the commencement of religious services in the long desecrated church of the Franciscans was in accordance with the altered mood of the Supreme Head of the Church of England. But this was as the flickering of the lamp in its socket. Before the close of the same month the great despoiler and small restorer lay dead in the palace of which he had deprived the archbishops of York.

[a] Both these documents are printed at length in Trollope's History of Christ's Hospital, 1834, 4to. Appendix, Nos. I. and II.

[b] See p. 53.

In the autumn of the same year the Reformers instituted a more rigorous visitation of churches than any that had previously taken place. All images were at that time pulled down throughout England, and all churches new white-limed.[a] At the same time all the altars in the church that was sometime the Grey Friars', with the walls and stalls of the choir, were removed and sold, and the whole reduced in length, in order to make it more consistent with the requirements of an ordinary parish church,[b] the arrangements for which were shortly after completed, the neighbouring churches of Saint Nicholas and Saint Ewen being removed.[c] All the tombs and large gravestones were at the same time [d] taken away, and sold for the paltry sum of fifty pounds, or thereabouts.[e] Amidst the general destruction of ancestral memorials which was accomplished in those days of heartless and impious spoliation, this act perhaps exceeded all others of the kind. The church of the Grey Friars had been the favourite place of sepulture with those of the aristocracy of England who had died in the metropolis. According to the reckoning of Weever the church had been honoured with the sepulture of

[a] See p. 54.

[b] The "west church," or nave, was afterwards rented to Henry Bolton, a schoolmaster, for 10*s*. per ann. See this and other particulars respecting the state of the church in Elizabeth's reign in Malcolm, iii. 333.

[c] See p. 55.

[d] From Weever's statement of this transaction it might be understood that it took place in 1545; for he says they were sold "by Sir Martin Bowes, Maior of London, An. 1545." Sir Martin was mayor in 1545: but Stowe's statement is that they were sold by Sir Martin Bowes, goldsmith and *alderman* of London; who evidently derived his authority to sell them, not as mayor, but in some other way. He was under-treasurer of the royal mint, and probably a commissioner for the sale of church property. The city might therefore employ him as a man of experience in such transactions It is asserted in Knight's London, vol. ii. 334, that Sir Martin "caused himself to be buried where he had set so bad a precedent;" but this is one of many errors in the article in that work on Christ's Hospital. Sir Martin Bowes was buried at St. Mary's Woolnoth.

[e] Stowe's Survay.

four Queens, four Duchesses, four Countesses, one Duke, two Earls, eight Barons,[a] and some thirty-five Knights: and in all six hundred sixty and three persons of quality. Stowe tells us that "there were nine tombs of alabaster and marble, invironed with strikes of iron, in the choir; and one tomb in the body of the church, also coped with iron; besides seven-score grave-stones of marble." Both Stowe and Weever derived their information from a catalogue of all the sepulchral monuments, made some time before the expulsion of the Friars, which is still preserved in their register, and which has been edited in the fifth volume of the Collectanea Topographica et Genealogica. This record is a very valuable one in a genealogical point of view. To the artistic antiquary it would have offered greater interest had it described the character of the monuments more fully; but it particularizes the "raised tombs," and they were more numerous than Stowe calculated. In the choir were those of queen Margaret the first foundress of the new church, of queen Isabella, of John earl of Pembroke, John lord Dynham, K.G., sir Robert Chalons, and Richard Hastings lord Willoughby and Welles. In the Lady chapel were those of Alice lady Kingston 1439, and sir Walter Langley 1470; in the chapel of the Apostles, south of the

[a] The Queens were, Margaret consort of Edward the First; Isabella consort of Edward the Second; Joan queen of Scots, daughter of Edward the Second; and Isabella queen of Man. Besides these the church had received the heart of a fifth queen, Alianor consort of Henry the Third, and also the heart of king Edward the Second, which was deposited under the breast of his queen's effigy. The Duchesses were but two: Beatrice duchess of Britany, daughter of king Henry III., and Alianor duchess of Buckingham, 1530; the Duke was the captive duke of Bourbon; the Earls were John Hastings earl of Pembroke, 1389, and Stowe adds the name of Roger Mortimer earl of March, beheaded in 1329, but which is not in the register; the Countesses were Margaret de Rivers countess of Devon, Margaret Marshal countess of Norfolk, 1389, (erroneously called a duchess by Stowe,) Isabella countess of Bedford, daughter of king Edward I.; and the lady reckoned by Weever as a fourth was probably Elizabeth lady Neville, mother of Ralph earl of Westmerland. It is, however, uncertain whether there was not also a countess of Menteith.

choir, was a great raised tomb of alabaster to sir Walter Blount knight of the garter 1474, and another to John Blount lord Mountjoy 1485; in the chapel of Saint Francis was a small raised tomb to sir John Robsard knight of the garter, and others to William Danvers under-treasurer of England 1439, sir Stephen Jennyns alderman of London 1523, and Hugh Acton citizen and taylor 1530; in the ambulatory, between the choir and altars, was an effigy of Theophania, the nurse and mistress of queen Isabella; and *coram altaribus* (probably at the eastern extremity of the church, like the Nine Altars at Durham) were raised tombs to sir John Devereux steward of the king's house, &c. K.G. 1385, John Norbury treasurer of England, Elizabeth lady Uvedale daughter of the last, and the lady Mountchensi, an effigy of temp. Edw. I. In the north aile was the raised tomb of William Harmer citizen and salter 1512, and in the south aile that of doctor John Tavlle chancellor of St. David's 1509. Such were some of the most conspicuous monuments; but the number of persons of distinguished character can only be estimated by perusing the catalogue itself.[a]

The Historian of Christ's Hospital has treated the grant of Henry VIII. as inoperative, and has asserted that during the early part of Edward's reign its provisions lay entirely dormant.[b] But this is altogether a mistake. Mr. Trollope was probably thinking only of his immediate subject, that is to say, a public school;

[a] Stowe, in his Survay, has enumerated the principal names, but his list is full of clerical errors.—During the excavations made on the site of the church of the Grey Friars about the year 1834, were found two ancient inscribed gravestones, which are not included among those catalogued in the Register. They commemorate Philip de Srepham, or Shropham, a monk of Ely, and Bernart de Jambe, probably one of the Italian merchants, of whom many were here interred. Etchings of these gravestones, which are preserved in the burial-ground of Christ church, have been made by Mr. E. B. Price, F.S.A.

[b] History of Christ's Hospital, by the Rev. William Trollope, 1834, 4to. pp. 30, 34.

but no such establishment was as yet in contemplation. The two parishes of Christ church and Saint Bartholomew's the Less were fully constituted by Henry's grant, and so was the control of the city over the hospital of Saint Bartholomew; and the city retained all the estates which the grant conveyed, neither receiving or requiring any subsequent confirmation of them from king Edward the Sixth. Among those estates was the late house of the Grey Friars, but with no specific instructions as to the purposes to which it should be devoted. Its disposal appears to have been left to the discretion of the citizens; by whom the measures proposed for the relief of the poor were kept in view, though possibly they were somewhat delayed in their execution. They in fact required time, and funds; for it was part of the original arrangement that the royal grants should be met by a general contribution from the citizens. Besides, the first measure accomplished was the hundred beds at St. Bartholomew's,[a] though those were soon found to be insufficient.

A commission was appointed by the king, and books were sent round to all the wards of the city, in order to collect contributions. This, as in more modern days, would occupy some time. On the 17th Feb. 1551-2, "the bookes of the reliefe of all the wards of London towards the new Hospitals" were received by the king's commissioners; and on that occasion the council dined with master Cowper the sheriff.[b]

In May 1552 we find bishop Ridley writing to secretary Cecill,[c]

[a] "The ordre of the Hospital of S. Bartholomewes in West-Smythfielde in London" is a curious little 12mo. volume of 70 leaves, printed "Londini. Anno 1552"—before the institution of the other city hospitals. It may be seen in the City Library at Guildhall.

[b] Stowe's Chronicle.

[c] The bishop's letter is printed in Strype's Stowe, fol. 1720, vol. i. p. 176, and in Trollope's Christ's Hospital, p. 37. At the same time the city presented a memorial to the privy council "to sue for the king's majesty's house at Bridewell," and unfolding the scheme of their proposed charities, which will be found in Malcolm's Londinium, ii. 554.

to state that the citizens were willing to provide for the poor "both meat, drink, clothing, and firing," but that they lacked lodging; wherefore he proceeded to beg "a wide, large, empty house of the king's majesty called Bridewell, that would wonderfully well serve to lodge Christ in,"—under which holy name, with much too free an adaptation of Matthew xxv. 35, 36, &c. the bishop was pleased to designate the poor, then "lying abroad, in the streets of London, both hungry, naked, and cold."[a] This application ultimately received a favourable reply, but not for nearly a year after.

Meanwhile, the citizens themselves did not cease in their exertions to mitigate the crying evil of a large houseless population. On the 26th July, 1552, began the preparing of the Grey Friars house for the poor fatherless children; and also, in the latter end of the same month, began the repairing of Saint Thomas's Hospital in Southwark, for poor impotent and lame persons.[b] This hospital had been an adjunct of the priory of Bermondsey, and had been purchased by the city of the crown, in 1550, as parcel of the lordship and manor of Southwark.

In the following month a fresh collection was set on foot. "This moneth of August began the great provision for the poore in London, towards the which every man was contributory, and gave certaine money in hand, and covenanted to give a certain [sum] weekly."[c]

[a] The same picture was graphically drawn by Thomas Lever, Master of St. John's college, in Cambridge, when he preached before the king on the fourth Sunday in Lent in 1550: "O merciful Lord! (he exclaimed) what a number of poor, feeble, halt, blind, lame, sickly,—yea, with idle vagabonds and dissembling caitiffs mixt among them, lye and creep, begging in the miry streets of London and Westminster!" It was not until the end of Elizabeth's reign, as is well known, that the parochial system of relief to the poor became the law of the land.

[b] Stowe's Chronicle.

[c] Ibid. An early account of the moneys collected is printed by Strype in his edition of Stowe's Survey, 1720, vol. i. p. 175, from the MSS. of archbishop Parker. The

In the course of four months the repairs at the Grey Friars were completed, and on the 23d of November the poor children were received, to the number of almost four hundred.[a] When the lord mayor and aldermen rode to Saint Paul's on the afternoon of the following Christmas day, all the children stood in array from Saint Laurence lane in Cheap towards Paul's, being 340 in number, attired in one livery of russet cotton,[b] the boys with red caps, and the girls with kerchiefs on their heads, having a woman-keeper between every twenty children, and accompanied also by the physicians and four surgeons, and the masters of the hospital—who were some of the most eminent citizens.[c]

On the 10th of April, 1553, the lord mayor was summoned to the court at Whitehall, where he received from the king's mouth an intimation that the appropriation of the royal manor-house of Bridewell place to the objects of a House of Occupation, or work-house, would be conceded, and that further the king would grant for the maintenance of that house, and for the hospital which the city had already undertaken at Saint Thomas's in Southwark, all the rents belonging to the Savoy hospital, which amounted to about 700 marks per annum, and also the beds and furniture of the Savoy,—which had been converted into a hospital by Henry the Seventh, but was now to be resumed by the crown.[d] This grant was accomplished

"whole Benevolence" of the citizens had amounted to 2,476*l.*; and the erection and furniture of the two houses (that is, St. Thomas and Christ's Hospitals) had been 2,479*l.* 10*s.* 10*d.*

[a] Stowe: see also the present Chronicle, p. 76.

[b] At the following Easter, Stowe described the boys as "all cloathed in plonket coates and red caps, and the mayden children in the same livery." Plonket was a blue colour: as Stowe himself explains this passage in his Survay—"and in Easter next they were in blue at the Spittle, and so have continued ever since."

[c] Stowe; the present Chronicle, p. 76; and Machyn's Diary, p. 28.

[d] The excuse made for discontinuing the hospital at the Savoy was that, though intended

by letters patent which passed the great seal on the 26th of June, within a shorter time of king Edward's death than that which had elapsed between the former grant and the death of king Henry. By these letters patent [a] it was directed that the three hospitals should in future be called "the hospitals of king Edward the Sixth, of Christ, Bridewell, and Saint Thomas the Apostle."

It is the pleasure of those who celebrate the origin of the school now called Christ's Hospital, to designate king Edward the Sixth as its special founder. Captivated with the beau-ideal of an amiable prince, a youth the patron of youth, a scholar the friend of scholars, such a theme, in such hands, has naturally amplified itself into a goodly Protestant legend, almost rivalling some of those of the earlier creed. An historical antiquary would receive little thanks if he ventured to brush rudely against the hallowed dew of so much loyal poetry and pious enthusiasm. Still, it will be evident from the preceding statement of facts that king Edward had very little to do with the foundation of Christ's Hospital. Both the house itself, and the revenues for its support, came from his predecessor, or were raised by the bounty of the citizens themselves; and we do not trace any thing bestowed upon it in Edward's letters patent beyond the name by which it should be known. And that is nothing more than occurred in scores of other instances throughout the country—many a grammar-school being named the school of Henry VIII. Edward VI. or Elizabeth respectively, merely because it was established (or in many cases remodelled) under authority derived from the sovereign.

for the lodging of pilgrims and strangers, it "was now made but a lodging of loyterers, vagabondes, and strumpets that lay all day in the fieldes, and at night were harbored there; the which was rather the maintenaunce of beggery than the reliefe of the poore." Grafton's Chronicle.

[a] Printed at length in Trollope's History of Christ's Hospital, Appendix No. V.

Moreover, Christ's hospital was not founded as a school; its object was to rescue young children from the streets, to shelter, feed, clothe, and *lastly* to educate them—in short, to do exactly what in later times has been done by each individual parish for the orphan and destitute offspring of the poor. Any high-flown eulogies upon Edward's love of learning are consequently in this case wholly misapplied. It does not appear that he even assisted in what the citizens were doing at the Grey Friars. All that can be affirmed is, that he was the founder of Bridewell hospital, and that he recognised Christ's hospital and St. Thomas's, which the citizens had already set on foot: the former having been originally their own foundation, and the latter having become their property by purchase.

The story runs that the king's attention was directed to this good work by a sermon preached before him by bishop Ridley in the year 1552: and that in consequence the king sent by the bishop a letter to the mayor, declaring his special commandment that the mayor should travail therein.[a] There is no reason to doubt that the sermon was preached, or that the amiable king was anxious to fulfil the part required of him: but this was not until after the citizens themselves had done what they could, and found that they required further aid from the crown. Bishop Ridley himself, in his farewell letter to his friends, written shortly before his martyrdom, attributed the chief merit to the city magistrates;[b] first to sir Richard Dobbs, in whose mayoralty

[a] Grafton.

[b] So long before as the mayoralty of Sir Richard Gresham in 1537-8, the year of king Edward's birth, the city had petitioned king Henry to have assigned to them the disposition and governance of the "iii. hospitalls or spytalls, commonly called Seynt Maryes Spytall, Seynt Barthilmewes Spytall, and Seynt Thomas Spytall, and the New Abbey of Tower-hill, founded of good devotion by ancient fathers, and endowed with great possessions and rentes, onely for the reliffe, comforte, and helpyng of the pore and impotent

the renewed effort was made, and who invited the bishop into the city council-chamber to advise with the aldermen thereon,—and next to his successor sir George Barnes, whose " endevour was to have a House of Occupation set up," and for that purpose procured the princely palace of Bridewell from " that godly king, that Christian and peerless prince."

Mr. Trollope tells us that "In the month of June, 1553, the young king received the corporation at the palace, and presented them with the charter, the children also being present at the ceremony."[a] This is purely legendary, as much so as the velvet coat and silver buttons which he says are among the archaic myths of the school-boys.[b] It was on the 10th of April, as already stated, that the king gave audience to the mayor. On the 26th of June, when the letters patent passed the seal, he was languishing in his last illness. Nor if he had lived on in health would he have delivered his charter to the corporation with the ceremonial represented. Mr. Trollope has adopted as a piece of contemporary evidence the great picture which hangs in the hall of Christ's hospital, not being aware of the element of poetry which it contains, stiff and ungainly as its composition

people, not beynge able to helpe themsellfes."—See this letter in Strype's Eccles. Memorials, i. 265; Trollope's Christ Hospital, p. 26; or Burgon's Life of Gresham, i. 26. By Trollope, " Seynt Maryes spytall " is misprinted " Seynt Georges." St. Mary's spital was without Bishopsgate, and at its surrender had nine-score beds, well furnished for receipt of poor people. (Stowe's Survay.)

[a] History of Christ's Hospital, p. 41.

[b] The blue-coat boys, it seems, indulge in some very amusing speculations on their now obsolete costume. " It has been imagined that the coat was the mantle, and the yellow, as it is technically called, the sleeveless tunic of the monastery; the leathern girdle also corresponding with the hempen cord of the friar. There is an old tradition among the boys, that the dress was originally of velvet, fastened with silver buttons, and an exact facsimile of the ordinary habit of their royal founder."—History of Christ's Hospital, p. 50.

seems to be—that it is in fact symbolical and not real in its incidents, and was painted long after the time supposed to be represented, probably in the following century.[a]

These remarks will not be thought wholly unnecessary, inasmuch

[a] This picture is usually attributed to Holbein, but in error. It is an amplification of Holbein's picture of the same subject, which is at Bridewell hospital. That picture contains only eleven figures, including the painter himself; the picture at Christ's hospital has ninety or more, and not only is it very inferior as a work of art, but obviously of posterior date in point of costume.

Holbein's picture at Bridewell, which must have been painted shortly before his death (if that event, as is generally supposed, occurred in London in 1554), is a highly valuable one, and a worthy companion to that which he painted for the Barber-Chirurgeons, representing their receiving their charter from Henry VIII. in 1541. The king is seated under a canopy of state, and delivers the charter with the great seal attached to the lord mayor, who with the two sheriffs kneels to his right hand. Behind them stand the lord chancellor (bishop Goodrich) and another attendant. To the left stand—a person in a laced gown, holding a roll in his hand, and supposed to be sir Robert Bowes the master of the rolls; and a nobleman wearing the garter, said to be the earl of Pembroke [but on what authority I do not know. One would rather imagine he might be the duke of Northumberland great master of the household, or lord Darcy the lord chamberlain.] Behind these are two other persons, undistinguished by their costume; and, next the edge of the picture, Holbein himself. A large engraving was made of this picture by Vertue in the year 1750.

The picture at Christ's hospital is derived from Holbein's so far as the principal figures go. The number of aldermen kneeling to the right is increased to eight; and to the left are bishop Ridley and three others also kneeling. In the background the governors of the hospital are standing with their wands, to the number of about forty. Besides these, a boy and girl of the hospital are kneeling before the king, and fourteen others of either sex are ranged in couples along the front of the picture, the rows being terminated by a beadle and a matron. This picture is very neatly engraved on a small scale by Mr. Augustus Fox, as the frontispiece to Mr. Trollope's History of Christ's Hospital. Its demerits are criticised " with candour " by Malcolm, who says the king's figure, though insignificant from its small size, is the only one whose attitude is easy, natural, and dignified. This is obviously because it is more faithfully copied than the rest from the Bridewell picture. Malcolm, however, had no suspicion that the picture at Christ's Hospital was not actually Holbein's work. My own impression is that it is of the period of James I. or Charles I.

There is also in the hall of Christ's Hospital a correspondent but still larger picture, in which king Charles the Second appears as the principal personage. This was painted by Verrio, chiefly at the instigation of Mr. Pepys. (Trollope, p. 124.)

as the "admirable description of the scene, preserved by one *who was no doubt an eye-witness*—the great painter Holbein,"—has already passed forth into our popular literature.[a] But still let us preserve our faith in the interesting anecdote related by Grafton and Stowe, that when the scheme for the endowment of the royal hospitals was placed before the pious prince, and, according to the usual practice, a blank had been left for the amount of property which it should be lawful for the city to hold in mortmain for this object, Edward with his own hand wrote in the sum, "four thousand marks by the year,"[b] and then exclaimed, in the hearing of his council, "Lord, I yield thee most hearty thanks that thou hast given me life thus long, to finish this work, to the glory of thy name!"[c]

Some of the buildings of the ancient convent, including the Fratry and Refectory, were standing in the early part of the present century.[d] The walls and windows of Whittington's Library were to be seen in a mutilated state on the north side of the cloisters, and there are many engravings which represent them.[e] Even now the southern walk of the friars' cloisters remains, and its pointed arches and buttresses may be seen from the exterior. The western walk of

[a] London, edited by Charles Knight, 1842, 8vo. vol. ii. p. 334. An expression of opinion follows that the scene is a real representation of the old palace at Westminster.

[b] King Henry's grant had limited the amount in the same place to one thousand marks.

[c] After which foundation established, adds Grafton, "he lived not above two days." This is probably a misprint for *ten* days. Edward lived exactly ten days after the date of the letters patent; but it would be to some earlier stage of the business that the anecdote (if literally true) would belong. It appears that the letters patent were preceded by an indenture between the King and the City, as in the case of the former royal grant. This indenture escaped the researches of Mr. Trollope; but Strype says it bore date in June, and he has given an abstract of it, from the register of the privy council, in his amplification of Stowe's Survey, (edit. 1720,) vol. i. p. 177; and also in his Ecclesiastical Memorials, vol. i. 425.

[d] Trollope, p. 105.

[e] Mr. Trollope's print, opposite p. 105, represents them restored.

the cloisters was under the Great Hall, which was pulled down in 1827, as was Whittington's Library about the same time.[a]

The Register of the Grey Friars of London is now bound as the latter part of the volume in the Cottonian Library marked Vitellius F. XII. It is of the size of a modern quarto book, and consists of 120 leaves of paper.[b]

The first thirty-two pages are occupied with a descriptive catalogue of the sepulchral monuments which existed in the church and cloisters, and the next eleven with an alphabetical index to the same. This catalogue, which was the authority for the summary and in many cases incorrect account of these monuments given by Stowe and Weever, was edited entire, by myself, in the fifth volume of the Collectanea Topographica, 1838, pp. 274—290, 385—398.

At fol. 316 of the present paging of the volume commences an historical account, in Latin, of the origin of the rule of Saint Francis, its introduction into England, and the foundation of the house of the fraternity in London, followed by an enumeration of the benefactions made to the house; at fol. 321 an account of the building of the convent and church;[c] at fol. 321 b. a description of the cistern and its watercourse; at fol. 323 "the founders of the new church;" at fol. 324 the contributors to the glazing of the windows; and at fol. 325 b an account of the foundation of the library, in the year 1421, by the worshipful *(venerabilis vir)* Richard Wyttyngton, mercer and mayor of London.[d] At fol. 326 is a curious English document, being "Indentures for the wyndoes of the south syde of the churche, and soo

[a] The shield of Whittington, within a quatrefoil, was inserted in various parts of this building. One of these carved stones is now in the museum of Mr. E. B. Price, F.S.A. and is represented in the etching at the end of this Preface.

[b] In the New Monasticon, vol. vii. p. 1514, it is erroneously described as being "on vellum."

[c] As already given in the notes, pp. xi.–xiii.

[d] See p. xiv.

to the farder gatte;" and at fol. 327 another indenture between the city, during the mayoralty of Whittyngton, and freer John Bruylle the warden, being the lease of an additional plot of ground. At fol. 329 is a catalogue of those Friars Minors who had suffered martyrdom; at fol. 330 a list of such as were bishops or confessors; at fol. 331 b. cardinals, members of the order; at fol. 332 a list of the Ministers General of the order; at fol. 334 a list of Ministers Provincial; at fol. 335 a list of those Friars Minors who had been kings and men of power in the world; at fol. 335 b. of those distinguished Englishmen who had entered the order; and at fol. 336 b. a few names of the most distinguished members of the Second and Third orders of Saint Francis. The whole of this very curious matter was extracted by Mr. John Stevens for his additions to Dugdale's Monasticon, and is printed in his first volume, pp. 112—125, professedly "faithfully translated from the *Latin* of that antient Manuscript, and what is there in *English* exactly transcrib'd, without varying from the Orthography." In the new edition of the Monasticon Anglicanum, vol. vi. pp. 1515—1522, the same matter is reprinted, so far as it relates to the London house, that is, to the close of the two indentures above described; but it is very much to be regretted that the opportunity was lost—possibly because the manuscript was then in a state of dilapidation from the Cottonian fire—to collate Stevens's copy, as, notwithstanding his professions of accuracy, his translation has frequent misconceptions of the sense of the original, and in the numerous proper names which are introduced it is continually incorrect. The first four names that occur are given—"Pugworth" *for* Yngworth, "Senonef" *for* Deuonensis, "Detrews" *for* Detreuizo, and "Monachetus" *for* Monacatus.[a] In

[a] These are the names of the four friars who first brought the rule of Saint Francis to

the next three pages there are more than thirty names more or less mistranscribed. In p. 113, l. 23, John Iwyn, the first benefactor of the house, is styled "citizen and physician" instead of mercer,[a] and the second benefactor is styled "John Fitzpiers" instead of Joyce (*Jocius*).

At fol. 337 commences the Chronicle which is printed in the present volume, and it extends to fol. 364 inclusive. The twenty-eight last leaves of the book are occupied with genealogies, combined with historical details, in the form of pedigrees. They commence with Adam, and proceed through the whole of the Scripture history; a branch conducts from Japhet, through Brute, Leir, &c. to the British kings; then follow the genealogies of the English kings of the various races before the Norman Conquest, and, last of all, those of more recent times to the death of Henry VIII. in 1546, and the accession of Edward the Sixth.

At fol. 326, after the account of Whittington's Library, is the following memorandum, made, as I presume, by the friar who compiled the Register, and who was probably then acting as librarian. It will be perceived that he writes in the first person. The date here given must be near the time of the original compilation of the book:

London (as before mentioned in p. x.): Richard Yngworth an English priest and preacher, Richard of Devonshire an English clerk of the order of acolytes and in age a youth, Henry of Treviso a Lombard and a layman, and Monacatus also a layman. The two former went on to Oxford, and founded the house of Franciscans there and also that at Northampton. See anecdotes of their adventures on their journey in the Monasticon under the Oxford house; only there the younger friar is called *Henry* of Devon.

[a] This and some others of Stevens's errors are followed in the introductory chapter of The History of Christ's Hospital, by the Rev. William Trollope (4to. 1834), who quoted the Cottonian Manuscript without inspecting it. The New Monasticon has changed the name of Iwyn into Edwin, and Malcolm has converted it into Swen.

after which the register of interments, and the chronicle of events, were probably entered regularly, as the materials arose.

"Memorandum quod frater Andreas Bavard sacræ theologiæ professor, anno Domini 1494°, videns chorum fratrum minorum Lond' minus bene instauratum libris choralibus. Mente concepi non posse elemosinas amicorum meorum melius expedire quam in libris scribendis choralibus ad laudem divinam et ad ejusdem divinæ laudis continuationem. Qua propter conduxit[a] .... unum scriptorem qui scripsit mihi unum legendarium in duabus partibus. Et unum antiphonarium in duabus partibus et unum psalterium et unum gradualem. Et alium impressum et in multis aliis reparavi. Et" (*after this a considerable space is left blank*).—Register, fol. 326.

I have before mentioned that the Register of the Grey Friars bears marks of having passed through the hands of John Stowe; and I have now to add that transcripts in his hand of the greater part of its Latin contents are preserved in the MS. Harl. 544.

Ut sciatur posicio canalium aqueductus fratrum minorum Lond'. (See p. xiii, note.)

Primo a limine portæ Johannis Sporon spacio trium pedum sub novo muro fratrum porreccio canalis in vicum versus Newgate quarenti occurrit. Semper autem dum in via jacet aquilonarem partem viæ tenet aliquantum et minus domos approximans sed quod rectitudo posicionis permittat. Sub porta de Newgate spacio .12. pedum profundatur, et directe extenditur sub muro cimeterii sancti Sepulchri exterius et ulterius, sed vici illius obliquacionem obliquatur ; juxta *lekewelle* protenditur, ibi bivium pertransiens buttat se contra fenestram domus Johannis Muchchethe, ibique curvatur versus pontem de Holeburne inter domum Willielmi Yrotheges et pontem ; ponitur sub aqua spacio .iij. pedum. Ultra rivulum illius aquæ circa spacium .viij. passuum juxta pontis murum ultra fracturam de industria factam ubi aqua plateæ descendit in loco semper lutoso. PRIMUM

---

[a] *Sic in orig. The next word is partly burnt off. Stevens has translated the passage* "I hired." *Stowe did not transcribe it.*

spurgellum latet sub terra spacio vero .iiij^or. pedum lapide marmoreo coopertum. Inde directe usque ad *liwrone lane* extenditur, ibique secundum rectitudinem venelle illius vel vici regirat ad aquilonem juxta occidentalem murum venellæ posicionem habens spacio distans iij. pedum. In fine autem illius venellæ a leva SECUNDUM spurgellum altitudine fere .vij. pedum et inde directe protenditur, campum transversando et sepes ad molendinum Thomæ de Basynges quod est proximum villæ. Ubi spacio .xviij. pedum profundatur. Ibi ex parte orientali molendini a latere aquilonis infra foveam tercium patet spurgellum. Inde spacium fero unius stadii ad occidentem parum vergendo ad aquilonem, occurrit sulcus unus viridius ab oriente in occidentem protentus et spinosus ad occidentem tortuosus latitudine fere .viij. pedum, terram dividens Johannis de Derkynge quæ jacet ex parte meridionali et terram Thomæ de Basynges quæ jacet ex parte aquilonari. IN ILLO autem sulco a capite orientali incipiendo .xvj. passus non saltus, et ibi a medio latitudinis sulci ubi signum ad hoc necessarium foret, verso vultu ad aquilonem directe super terram Thomæ de Basynges spacio pedum xiiij. latet sub terra spacio .iiij. pedum CAPUD aquæ quod propinquius est, unde pro majore parte aquam habemus, parum autem de capite remociori. AB ILLO autem loco directe extenditur ad capud quod remocius est versus occidentem, cujus domuncula lapidia a remoto videtur. Aqua autem istius capitis adducitur ultra foveam Thomæ de Basynges a parte occidentis a latere aquilonis aliquantulum spacio a domo capitis circa .xv. passuum juxta viam quæ dividit inter parochiam sancti Egidii et sancti Andreæ. Ista aqua in domo capitis illius descendendo ad canalem super effluit et a canali parum vel nil inde recipitur ; set domum totam inundat, et per rivulos et rimas parietis negligenter amittitur. Apponat remedium, fratrum considerans dampnum et amissionem tot sumptuum.

NOTE.—*Liwrone lane* is called *Lither lane* by Stowe, and *Leather lane* by Strype in 1720. There is or was a small street called Windmill street running into it, perhaps marking the site of Thomas of Basynges' mill. At no great distance, in the low ground, were several water-mills, which gave name to Turnmill street, leading from Smithfield towards Clerkenwell. The stream, as Stowe tells us, was called Turnmill brook, or the River of Wells, for there were many natural springs near at hand. It was the navigable part only of this stream, from Holborn bridge to the Thames, that was properly " the Fleet," and latterly called Fleet Ditch.

E. B. PRICE F.S.A. sc.

ARMS OF SIR RICHARD WHITTINGTON,

from the Library of the Grey Friars.

A. D. 1421.

THE CHRONICLE

OF THE

GREY FRIARS OF LONDON.

RICARDUS PRIMUS REX.

Kynge Rychard the Furst surnamed Cure de Lyon was crownyd the iij^{de} daye of September, the yere of our Lorde God M^{l}clxxxix, the furst yere of hys rayne.

P^{i}.^{o}. A^{o}. Thys yere beganne the order of our Lady in Pruce.[a]

And this yere the Jues ware commandyd owte of Ynglonde.

vij^{o}. A^{o}. In this yere the kynge went in to the holy londe, and toke the citte of Akers, Porth . . . and Babilon, the yere of our lorde God M^{l}clxxxxvj.

viij^{o}. A^{o}. In this yere was one William with the long berde taken out of Bowe churche and put to dethe for herysey.

ix^{o}. A^{o}. In this yere beganne the order of the Trenyte.

x^{o}. A^{o}. In this yere this nobull kynge and great warryar dyssesyd in France comynge homward, by the hurte of a qwarrelle the iij^{de} daye of September; and his harte byrryd at the hye auter at Rome [Rouen], and hys body at Fonteverard.

[a] Called "The order of seynt Tonyes in Pruce," in the Chronicle of London, MS. Harl. 565, edited by Sir Harris Nicolas, 4to. 1827.

JOHANNES REX.

Kynge Johan, brothar unto Rychard, was crownyd upon the Assencion daye, the yere of our Lord God M[l]clxxxxix.

P[i].°. In this furst yere he lost Normandy and Angeoy, and every ploughe lond tasked at iij[s] for to gete it a gayne.

ij°. A°. Thys yere was chosyn by the wyse men of the citte of London xxxv. men, and sworne to mayntayne the assies in London.

iiij°. A°. Thys yere felle gret raynes, and gret thunder, lytenyng, and hayle-stones as grete as eggys, that dystroyd cornes [and] fruttes; and fowlles seying[a] flyeng in the eyer berynge burnynge coles, and brent many huses *(sic)*. And that yere the londe was enterdyted.

vj°. A°. Thys yere began the order of Freer Prechars. And then was a grete wynter of frost and colde that lastyd from new-yeres daye unto our lady day the Annunciacion.

vij°. A°. This yere alle pleys longynge un to the crowne ware pletyd at the tower of London.

ix°. A°. Thys yere the londe was interdytyd. And this same yere was borne Henry the [eldest] sonne to kynge John. And this yere beganne the names of mayeres and shreffys in the citte of London.

xj°. A°. Thys yere the londe was reconciled, and the interdyction relesyd.

xiij°. A°. Thys yere was grete dyscencione betwene the kynge and hys lordes; and Lewys the kynges sonne of France dyd moch harme in Ynglond. Southewarke the bregge with moch of the citte was brent.

xv°. A°. Thys yere at Candelmas the kynge sheppyd at Porthes-mothe, and sayled to Peytoe.[b]

xvj°. A°. Thys yere beganne the Freer Minors in Ynglond.

[a] *This word should be* seen. Compare a similar passage in Nicolas's Chronicle of London.

[b] Poictou.

xvij°. A°. Thys yere this king John was powsynd at Worster; and whane he hade raynyd xvij. yeres he dyde, and is burryd there in the monkes before the hye auter.

HENRICUS TERTIUS REX.

And here beganne the rayne of kyng Henry the third, sonne unto kynge John.

Pi.°. A°. Thys yere was Walis interdityd. And Lewys of France had one thousand marke of sylver for his rewarde.

ij°. A°. Thys yere the kynge had of every plough land Cs. And the same yere Thomas Becket removyd uppe behynde the hye auter in Christes church in Canterbery.[a]

v°. A°. Thys yere the kyng Henry the third was crownyd at Glossytor.[b] And alle pleys longynge to the crowne was pletyd in the tower of London. And the castelle of Bedford was destroyed. And this yere, on sent Lewys daye, was soch a stronge wynde in the north-est that it overturnyd houses, toweres, trees, and in the ayre was sene fyere draggons and sprettes flyenge. And this yere began the ordere of the Freeres Carmelyttes.

vij°. A°. Thys yere came the Freeres Minors into Ynglond. And a man of Oxenford feynyd hym to be Cryst, and was crucifyed at Addurbury.

xl°. A°. Thys yere a Jew felle in to a drawte on a satorday, and he wolde not be draune owte that day for the reverens of hys sabbot day, and sir Richard Clare, that time tyme beynge erle of Gloucseter,[c] seynge that he wolde not be drawne owte that day, he wolde

[a] This refers to the removal of the body of Becket from the undercroft of the church, where it was at first interred, to the shrine prepared for its reception in the new chapel of the Trinity. This event was afterwards annually celebrated as the Translation of the saint, upon the 7th July. See Pilgrimages of Walsingham and Canterbury, 1849, p. 224.

[b] King Henry was crowned for the second time this year, but it was at Westminster. His first coronation took place at Gloucester, shortly after the death of his father.

[c] Other chronicles which contain this story relate that it took place at Tewkesbury, where the earl of Gloucester was lord of the town.

not suffer hym to be drawne owte on the sonday, for the reverens of the holy sonday, and soo thus the false Jue perished and dyde therein.

liv^{o}. A^{o}. Thys yere this kynge Henry the thirde dyde, and ys burryd at Westmynster on sent Edwardes daye the marter.

EDWARDUS PRIMUS REX.

And then beganne the rayne of hys sonne kynge Edward the furst, that was callyd kinge Edward with the longshangkes.

xxv^{o}. A^{o}. Thys yere kynge Edward toke the castelle of Eddynbrow, the cheffe regalles in Scotlond, his crowne and hys cepter, and browte it to Westmyster, and offerd it un to sent Edwarde, the morrow after sent Bothols day, the yere of our lorde M^{l}.cc.iiij^{xx}.xvij^{o}.

xxxij^{o}. A^{o}. This yere the order of the Templers ware dystroyd thorowte alle cristyndome in one daye.

xxxv^{o}. A^{o}. Thys yere dyde kynge Edward the furst, and is burryd at Westmyster.

EDWARDUS SECUNDUS REX.

And here beganne the rayne of kynge Edwarde the second, that was borne at Carnarvan, and is called Edward of Carnarvan.

ix^{o}. A^{o}. Thys yere a bushelle of wett was at five shillings.

xix^{o}. A^{o}. Thys yere dyde kynge Edward Carnarvan, the wych marryd the eyer of France, by the wych qwene the flower de lyce came in to the armes of Yenglond, and the tyttyll of France; the wych kynge lyeth burryd at Glosceter.

EDWARDUS TERTIUS REX.

And here begynnyth the rayne of kynge Edward the third, borne at Wynsore, the yere of our Lorde 1327.

iij^{o}. A^{o}. Thys yere was Roger Mortemer erle of March hangyd and drawne at Tyborne for treson.

vij°. A°. Thys vijth yere of this kynge was the towne and castelle of Barwyke yelded up to the kynge. And in thys tyme was the order of the knyghttes of the garter made furst.

xij°. A°. [This yere the kynge chang]ed hys armes and made a newe qwyne, as the nobylle, halfe nobylle, and ferdy[ng noble. This] yere was the battelle of Sklyice. And thys yere was gret deth of men and bestes; and wh[eat dear, for a qu]arter of whett was solde for xl s.

xiv°. A°. Thys yere was the battelle in the Slewse havyne with sheppes. And this yere the kynge . . . .

xvij°. A°. This yere was a gret yerth qwake.

xx°. A°. This yere was the battell of Grece.[a]

xxj°. A°. Thys yere the kinge wan Callys. And this yere the xj. day of September was the battelle of Durham, wher kyng David of Scotland was tane.

xxiij°. A°. Thys yere was a gret pestelens in Yenglond.

xxv°. A°. Thys yere was the Spanyche battelle abowte Romney and Wynchelsey.

xxx°. A°. Thys yere the prince Edward toke the kynge of France, and the battell of Peyters.

xxxv°. A°. Thys yere was the second grete pestelens. And this yere the xiiij. day of Aprill, the wyche was the monday after Ester day, the kyng beyng with hys pepulle at Paris, seyng the daye so colde and derke that moche of hys pepulle dyde, it was callyd the blacke monday. And then dyde dame Blanche duches of Lankester.

xxxvij°. A°. Thys yere was a grete wynde on sent Maury's daye that dyd moche harme in many places. And Henry that was duke of Lankester dyde.

xl°. A°. This yere in Januarij Adam Bury was dyschargyd of hys mayrehod by the commandment of the kyng, and John Lowken was chosyn in his rome.

[a] Cressy.

xlij°. A°. Thys yere was the kynge of Spayne tane by the prince, and the erle of Dene [a] and . . aythn Claykyne [b] ware taken. And this yere was the iij. great pestelens.

xliij°. A°. Thys yere was a grete warre in France by sir Roberte Knowlles knyght.

xliiij°. A°. Thys yere was a grete dere yere.

xlvij°. A°. Thys yere was one John Norwelde mercer of London slayne at Blackehethe at a wrestlynge.

lj°. A°. Thys yere was John Mysterworth drawne and hangyd. And this yere dyde kyng Edwarde, and is burryd at Westmyster.

RICARDUS SECUNDUS REX.

And here beganne the rayne of kynge Richard the ij[de], sonne unto kyng Edward the iij[de].

ij°. A°. Thys yere one Hall a sawere [c] of the kynges was slayne in Westmyster church, and Sakke hys fellow was arestyd and put in to the towere of London by sir Alyne Buxhylle constabulle of the tower and by sir Raffe Ferres by fore the erle of Dene.[d]

iiij°. A°. Thys yere came iiij. galys to Gravysende, and brent a parte of the towne. And this same yere, on corpus Christi daye, was the rysynge of Kent and Essex, and they ware callyd Jake Strawes men, and came to London, and brent the Savoy and a parsell of sent Jones at Clarkenwell, and went to the tower of London, and there toke owte sir Simond Beuerle [e] archebyshoppe of Cantorbury and chaunsler of Yenglond, Robert Halys prior of sent Jones, freer William Appultone a gray freer, and dyvers other, and beheddyd them at the towere hyll, and slew manny Flemynges and

[a] The count de Dene, a noble Spaniard, at the battle of Najara.

[b] Sir Bertram de Claicon, a Norman. (Fabyan.)

[c] Sewer? *or* Squire?

[d] This affair had to do with the count de Dene the Spanish prisoner before mentioned: see the facts related by Mr. Beltz in his memoir of Sir Alan Buxhull, K.G., in Memorials of the Garter, p. 190.

[e] An error for Sudbury.

other men. Thys yere also was the grete yerth-qwake. And this yere the qwene Anne, the emperores dowter of Rome, came to Dover, and was crownyd at Westmyster, and weddyd unto the most excellent prince kynge Richard ij[de] on Fabian and Sebastian daye, and the coronacion on sent Vinsenttes daye followynge.

viij°. A°. John More was arestyd whyle he was shreffe.

ix°. A°. Thys yere sir Edmonde Langle and sir Thomas Wodstoke ware made duckes, [and sir] Myhyll at Pole [and] sir John Ormonde ware made erles at Westmyster.

xj°. A°. Thys yere Alexander Nevell archbyshoppe of Yorke, Roberte Vere ducke of Ireland, Myhell Poole erle of Suffoke, Roberte Trevelyan justyce, and Nicolas Breme knyght and alderman of London, ware a peched of treson by sir Thomas ducke of Glociter, Richard erle of Arnedell, and sir Thomas erle of Warwyke; and the foresayd Roberte of Vere chalynched them in the felde and was overcome, and the sayd Myghell, Robert Trevelyan, Nicolas Breme, Thomas Blacke, John Urke clerk, and John Saulsbury knyght, ware drawne and hangyd, and Simond Burle, John Bewchamp, and James Biernes, knyghtes, and others, be heddyd at towre-hyll for treson.

xiij°. A°. Thys yere was another grete pestelens in Yenglande.

xiiij°. A°. Thys yere the goodman at the Cooke [a] in Cheppe, at the new condite in Cheppe, was morderd in hys bede by nyght, and the wyffe of the howse brente and three of hys servanttes drawne and hanged at Tyborne for the same dede.

xv°. A°. Thys yere at Mydsomer, John Hynde [mayor] was dyscharged by the kinges councelle, and [the] shreffes. Edward Deckengton knyghte was made mayor, Edward [b] Maghfelde [and] Thomas Newton shreffes. And in July followyng the sayd mayer was dyschargyd, and for hym was schosyn Baudwyn Radyngton. And at sent Edwardes day was schosyn, as it aperys here followyng, [William Standon mayor and Gilbert Maghfelde and Thomas

[a] Cock ?

[b] *This should be* Gilbert.

Newton sheriffs.] And this yere was the citte of London raunsomed at a C.M[l]. marke.

xvj°. A°. In thys yere was the terme removyd from Westmyster unto Yorke from the fest of sent John Baptyst un to Crystmas.

xvij°. A°. Thys yere qwene Anne dessecyd, and is burryd at Westmyster.

xviij°. A°. Thys yere the Iryche men in August were commandyd home by the kynges commandment.

xx°. A°. Thys yere dyde Mare the countes of Derby. And in June dysscessid the mayer, and for hym was schosyne Richard Wyttyngton and occupied un tyll sent Edwardes daye. And this yere qwene Isabell the kynges dowter of France was weddyd un to kynge Richard at Callys. And thys yere dyde sir Thomas Woodstoke duke of Glosceter at Callys.[a] And the erle of Arundelle was be heddyd at towre hylle. And thys yere Henry erle of Derby enterd in to Yenglond at Ravynspore in Yorkeshere. And this yere dyde John duke of Langkester [on] sent Blace day, and lythe burryd at Powlles. And this yere was Busshe, Bagot, Scroppe, Grene, with others, ware be heddyd at Brystowe. And thys yere was the grete parlame[nt.]

xxj°. A°. Thys yere was restyd the duke of Glosceter and sent to Callys to prisone. And the morrowe after holy-rode daye the kynge made a gret justynge be syde Kyngstone uppon Temes.

In September was the erle of Arnedelle jugyd to deth, and sir Thomas Mortemer the same, but if he came in within iij. monythes; and the erle of Warwyke was juggyd to the same jugment as the erle of Arnedelle had, but he submyttyde hym selfe, and the kynge gave hym hys lyffe, and send hym un to the tower agayne; and then the parlament was removyd un to Shrowesbery; and that daye was made five dukes and a markes and four erles;

[a] In this and the following events crowded into this year there is nothing but error. They belong to the two following years, in which they are entered again. And Bagot was not beheaded at all: on this misapprehension, which is common to many chroniclers, see some remarks in the Gentleman's Magazine for March, 1849.

the names the erle of Darby duke of Hereforde, the erle of Rotlonde duke of Aumarlde, erle of Kent duke of Surrey, erle of Huntyngtone duke of Excetor, erle Marchalle duke of Norfoke, and the countes of Norfolke duches of Norfolke, earle of Somerset markes Dorcet, lorde Spencer erle of Gloceter, lorde Nevelle erle of Westmerlond, Thomas Perce erle of Welchere,[a] William Scroppe erle of West-chester.[b] And that same tyme dyde the lorde Mombray, and is byryd at the Whyt Fryers.

xxij°. A°. Thys yere dyde the duke of Lankester. And sir William Bagot was arestyd in Irelond and browte to London to Newgate. And duke Henry of Langkester entered into Inglond in Yorkechere at Ravyns-spurre be-syde Welyngtone.[c] And sir William Scroppe, sir Henry Grene, and sir John Busshe beheddyd at Brystow. And thys yere the kynge was deposyd by the comyns of his pepulle, and for hyme came Henry the iiij[th], that was erle of Darby.

HENRICUS QUARTUS REX.

P[io]. A°. Thys yere Ewene Glendore sqwere of Wallys made warre ayenst the kynge. The furst yere of his rayne was be-heddyd at Cerceter[d] the erle of Saulsbery [and] the erle of Kente, and at Oxenforde sir Thomas Blont, sir Benet Ely,[e] knyghttes, Thomas Wynter[f] sqwere, and sir John Holond erle of Huntyngton was be-heddyd at Plasshe in Essex, and their heddes sett on London brygge, and sir Barnarde Brokkas knyght was be-heddyd at London in Cheppesyde, and sir Thomas Shellé knyght, Maud-lyne and Feryby clarkes, ware hangyd at Tyborne. This same yere the kynge rode towerd Scotlond.

ij°. A°. Thys yere the qwene Isabelle that was wyffe to kynge

[a] *This should be* Worcester.

[b] *And this* Wiltshire.

[c] *An error apparently for* Bridlington.

[d] Cirencester.

[e] Sely *in other chronicles*.

[f] Wintercell *or* Wintershall.

Richard was sent home in to France owte of Yenglond. And that yere was a qwarter of whett at xvj[s]. the second dere yere. And that yere was a prest brent in Smythfelde that was callyd sir William Sautre for erysse.

iiij[o]. A[o]. Thys yere was the qwene crownyd.

v[o]. A[o]. Thys yere the byshoppe of Yorke, Scroppe, and Mowbray the earl marchall,[a] beheddyd. And three men of the kynges chamber hongyd, and the prior of Lau[nde], sir Robert Claryndon knyght, and eight freer minores ware hongyd at Ty[burne]. And thys yere was the battelle of Shrewysbery, in the wyche was slayne Henry Percy and Thomas Percy taken, and two dayes kepte, and after was honged and be-heddyd and hys hede with one qwarter of Henry Percy set on London brygge. And in this battelle was slayne the erle of Stafforde under the kynges banner. And this battelle was on Mary Mawdlyne evyn. And in the lent afore was the blasynge sterre that clarkes callyd it *stell.. cemate.*[b] And William Serle that was cheffe yomane with kynge Richard was drawne and honged and heddyd at Tyborne, and the qwarters saltede.

vij[o]. A[o]. Thys yere one Travers, a yoman of the crowne of the kynges, was hongyd at Tyborne for powsenynge of hys wyffe and one Pylle in the counter in the Powltre. And this yere alle the kydelles[c] and trungkes thorowghout the Temse from the towne of Stanes in the west unto the watter of Medevey in the est by the mayer and commonalte of London were dystrowyd and brent, and gret plee and dyscorde was for that matter betwene Thomas Arundelle archebyshoppe of Canterbery and other lorddes and knyghtes on that one party, and the mayor and commonalte of London on that other party, but the citte of London recovered their ryght by the vertu of the kynges charter and hys statues. Thys yere also was many justes in Smytfelde by-twene Englyche

[a] *Blundered in the MS. to* Mombre Kerrelle. [b] *Stella comata.*

[c] For catching fish : called "weares" in the parallel passage of Stowe's Chron.

men and Scottes, and by-twene lordes and knyghttes of Ynglonde and other strangers. And this yere was the erle of Arundelle weddyd at Lambyth.[a] And this yere was furst ordened a masse of the Holy Gost, to be songe solemply be note every yere at the Yelde-halle chappelle the same daye the mayer is chosyn.

viij°. A°. Thys yere the erle of Northumberlond and the lorde Bardolfe was be-heddyd in the North; and the erles hede with one of hys qwarters of the lordes *(sic)* ware sett on London bregge. And this yere sir Roberte Knowlles knyghte dyde, that was the grete warryar. And this yere sir Thomas Rampsone knyghte of the garter[b] was drowned in the Temse by hys owne follé, for he wolde not be governyd by the bargemen, but to have hys owne rewle. And this yere was the erle of Kent weddyd at sent Mary Overes.[c]

xj°. A°. Thys yere was ordened the alay of golde. And the kynges sonnes beten in Chepe.[d] And this yere was the grete frost and ise and the most sharpest wenter that ever man sawe, and it duryd fourteen wekes, so that men myght in dyvers places both goo and ryde over the Temse. Thys yere also was the good erle of Kent slayne [at] the castelle of Brydoke in Bryttene with a qwarrelle in hys hede. And thys yere was an erytyke brentte in Smythfelde for eryse. And a sqwere of [Wa]llys, one heghe Rys de 9de,[e] draune and hongyd for tresone.

[a] Thomas earl of Arundel married Beatrix illegitimate daughter of John I. king of Portugal: upon the morrow after the feast of St. Katharine in 6 Hen IV. (viz. 26 Nov. 1404) as recorded by Walsingham. Ypodigma Neustriæ, p. 175. See also Tierney's History of Arundel, p. 283, and the Collectanea Topogr. et Geneal. vol. i. pp. 80 et seq.

[b] Sir Thomas Rempston, elected K.G. in 1400; he was constable of the tower of London at the time of his fatal accident, which occurred on the 31st Oct. 1406.

[c] Edward Holand, fourth earl of Kent, married Lucia, daughter of the duke of Milan; see Leland's Collectanea, i. 698. He was killed at Briac in Britany on the 15th Sept. in the following year.

[d] "In this yere was a fray made in Estchepe, be the kynges sones Thomas and John, with men of the town." Chron. of London (Nicolas), p. 93. The prince of Wales, it seems, was not engaged in this memorable fray: but Shakspere has made him bear the sins of his younger brethren.

[e] Ryse ap Dee *in other chroniclers.*

xij°. A°. Thys yere there came a cardinelle to London. And menny justes and battelles ware in Smythfelde. And this yere beganne a gret pley from the begynnyng of the worlde at the skynners' welle, that lastyd vij. dayes contynually; and there ware the most parte of the lordes and gentylles of Ynglond.[a] And this yere was a goldsmythe of Fletestret slayne be nyght in the dukes place of York with-owte Tempull barre, and was trowne[b] under the Tempull bregge.

xiij°. A°. Thys yere was a gret excesseve flode in the Temse. And a gret batte [battle] rose betwene Roberte Glocitre and Arthur Ormesby in Smythfelde. And this yere the lorde Thomas weddyd the countes of Somerset.[c] And this yere came messengeres owte of France from the kynge and the duke of Burgone for to helpe them agaynst the duke of Orlyans; and then went over the erle of Arnedelle and the erle of Kent to helpe the duke of Burgone, and had a jurné, and came home agayne; and that same tyme came messengeres owte of France from the duke of Orlians for to have helpe agayne the duke of Burgayn.

xiv°. A°. Thys yere the xx^{ti} day of March, dyde the kynge, and was burryd at Cantorbery.

HENRICUS QUINTUS REX.

And kyng Henry the Fifth was crownyd, that was hys sonne, at Westmyster the ixth day of April, the yere of our lorde God M^{l}cccc xiij.

P^{io} A°. Thys yere the lorde Cobhame made a rysynge with many lollars and heryttykes, as Roger Actone and many moo, to the number of xxxvj.; and ware draune and hangyd on a gallows new

[a] Stowe places this great play under the year 1409. See also other chronicles quoted in Collier's Hist. of Dramatic Poetry, i. 19.

[b] thrown.

[c] Thomas of Lancaster duke of Clarence and Margaret (Holand) widow of John Beaufort earl of Somerset.

made in sent Gylles felde, and five of them ware brent, the kynge lyinge at sent Jones.[a]

ij°. A°. Thys yere the kynge wanne Harflew in Normandy. And this yere Richard Gurmon,[b] French baker of Lumberstreth, was brent in Smythfelde. And this yere was the kynges grete worke begonne at Shene. And this yere the kynge toke his viage towarde Normandy, and rode thorow the citte of London unto Sowthhamtone the xviij. day of June, and there he abode, his stoffe, and hys company. And the v. daye of August nexte ware put to deth at Hamton sir Richard of Yorke erle of Chambrych, the lorde Scroppe, and sir Thomas Grey knyght, for treson, imagenynge the kynges deth. And in this tyme was one Claydon[c] skenner brente in Smythfelde the xth. day of September. And the morrow after sent Laurens day the kynge with hys pepulle sheppyd at Porchemowth, and he landyd at Kedecause, three myle owte of Harflew, on our lady day the Assumpcion. And the kynge layd hys sege fro that daye unto the xxij. daye of September or the towne ware yelded up. And in that whyle there dyde manny of hys pepull, as the erle of Surye,[d] the byshope of Norwyche,[e] sir John Phylpot, and many other knyghttes and sqweeres, and a grete many of the comyn pepulle. And then the towne and castelle was yeldyd up unto the kynge with the keyes, and the kynge made the lord Bewforde[f] that was erle of Worseter captayne. And thene the kyng toke [his] waye towerd Callys with viij.M^{l}. fyghtynge men. And the xxv. day of October on sent Crispians day the lordes and chevaltre of France layd with xxvj. M^{l}. men, and wolde have stoppyd the kynges waye, that he shulde not passe to Callys. And the kynge with his host batellyd with them manfully, and fowght with theme

[a] The priory of St. John's at Clerkenwell.

[b] Turmyne, a heretic. Chron. Lond. (Nicolas).

[c] John Claydon. (Ibid.)

[d] Thomas Arundel, more commonly called earl of Arundel; he returned home sick of the dysentery, and died at his own castle of Arundel, on the 13th of Oct. 1415.

[e] Richard Courtenay bishop of Norwich died at the siege of Harfleur, 20 Sept. 1415.

[f] Richard Beauchamp lord Abergavenny, afterwards earl of Worcester.

in a felde called Agyncort, and slew and toke of them dukes, erles, and knyghttes and other to a grete number, and a grete multytewde of the comyn pepulle. And of Englyche men was slayne, as the duke of Yorke, the erle of Sur[ry [a]], and other, but a fewe. And the morrow after Simond and Jude daye tydynges came to the new mayer of the sodyne battelle. And then was made grete solempnites and processions was done ther for, with prelattes, prestes, freeres, and other sage men of the cytte. And after that the kynge came to Dover, Cantorbery, and soo to London; and there the mayer, aldermen, comyns, rydynge worshyppully ayenst hym in rede gownes and whyte hoddes, and browte hym to Westmyster. Also this yere came the emperar of Almen [b] in to Ynglond with viij C. hors to sent Georges felde. And the xxix. day of March the duke of Holonde [c] came to London, and he laye at the byshoppe of Elys place in Holborne.

iiij°. A°. Thys yere the xiiij. day of December sir John Oldecastell knyghte was drawne from the tower of London un to sent Gylles in the felde and there was hongyd and brent. Thys yere one sent Martyns day was byshoppe Martyne the vth. chosyne byshoppe of Rome.

vj°. A°. John Briane was drowned in hys shrefehode, and in his stede was chosyne John Perneys shreffe for the resydew of the yere. And this yere on sent Donstons day was the towne of Rome yeldene to the emperor; and the towne of Ponteys was taken, with many other castelles and towers.

vij°. A°. Thys yere the qwene Katerne was crownyd the xxij. day of Marche.

[a] Not slain in the battle, as stated in the preceding passage.

[b] The emperor Sigismond came to England, and was installed as a knight of the garter on the 7th May, 1416. He was brother to Anne the queen of Richard the Second.

[c] William of Bavaria count of Ostrevant, who had been formerly admitted into the order of the garter by king Richard II. in 1390, came to meet the emperor; but, having been detained by contrary winds, did not arrive until the 28th of May (not March).—Beltz, Memorials of the Garter, p. 340. "The counts of Holland of this family, being by birth dukes of Bavaria, were usually styled *dukes* of Holland."—Ibid.

ixo. Ao. Thys yere the towne of Mewys in Bry was yeldyn.

And this yere Mortemer brake owte of the tower of London, and was takyn agayne afterward in Walys, and browte agayne un to the tower of London. And this yere was browte to London a byshoppe, a knyght, and a captayne of Mewys in Bry, with xxviij. prisoners of France. And this yere was the furst provincialle chapter of freeres minors in London. And this yere the kynge dyssecyd,

HENRICUS SEXTUS REX.

and hys sonne Henry the vjth beganne his rayne.

P^{io} A^{o}. Thys yere Newgate was new made by master Richard Wyttyngtone, and he dyde the same yere.

ij^{o}. A^{o}. Thys yere the xxij. day of Februarij was draune and hongyd and behedyd and qwarterd Mortymer for treson. And this yere the prince of Portyngale came in to Englonde.

iij^{o}. A^{o}. Thys yere was a grete debate betweene the cardnalle of Wenchester and the duke of Glosater and the citte of London.

And this yere came v. gallys to London with marchandes.

v^{o}. A^{o}. Thys yere was one hongyd, heddyd, and qwarterde at Tyborne Segewyke.

vj^{o}. A^{o}. Thys yere was the concelle of Redynge. And this yere dyde Thomas duke of Exceter. This yere was Wylle Wawe hongyd at Tyborne.

viij^{o}. A^{o}. Thys yere the kynge was crownyd. And Jake Stawe was hongyd and qwarterd.[a] And this yere was a grete stronge fyer at Banyscastell[b] the xvij. day of October that brent a grete parte, and dyd moche harme. And this yere dyde the good erle [of] Salsburry sir Thomas Mountagew at Orlians in France.

x^{o}. A^{o}. And this yere was ane herytyke brent at towre hylle

[a] This clause of the MS. is erased by the hand of John Stowe, who has written the words "at Westmystar" instead.

[b] Baynard's castle, in the city of London.

the xxiiij. day of Janivare. And in the morrow after there was a grete battelle in Smythfelde betwene Upton and John Downe; and whan they had fowth longe, the kynge toke up the matter and gave them grace. And Thomas Bagley viker of Mundene[a] in Essex was dysgradyd and brent in Smythfelde. And this yere[b] the kynge was crownyd the xvj. day of December in Paries solemply, and the ix. day of Februarij he came to Dover, and the xxj. daye of the same monythe he came to London, and there was worchippfully reseved of the cittesens in whytt gownes and redde whoddes.

xj°. A°. Thys yere was the grete cowncell at Baselle, and many lowlers dystroyd in Pruce.[c] And this yere John duke of Bedforde and the regent of France came to Callys be-fore Ester; and the morrow after there ware sodiers arestyd and prisond, and in the Ester weke the duke rode toward Picardy in Tyrwyne. And thene the byshoppe of Tyrwyne weddyd the duke and the erle of sent Powlys dowghter to-gether; and then they came to Callys, and on sent Barnardes day iiij. sodiers ware be-heddyd and a C & x. of the other sodiers ware exiled.[d] And on mydsomer evyn the duke with hys wyffe came to London.

xij°. A°. Thys yere was a grete pestelens, and a grete frost. And the duke of Bedford dyde, and lyth at Rome.[e] And this yere abowte wytsontyde the lowlers of Prage ware dystrowyd, soo that in two battelles there ware slayne xx.M[l]. with their captayns, and there was tane one master Pers clarke, and another Englych herytyke, enimys to alle holy churche.

xiij°. A°. Thys yere in harvest was the cowncelle in Arays that pesse shulde be reformyd be-twene Yngland and France, and there ware lordes both spiritualle and temporalle. And thether came the

[a] Manuden: see Newcourt's Repert. ii. 403.

[b] day *in MS.*

[c] Lollards in Prussia.

[d] Compare this with the account of the duke's proceedings at Calais in Chron. of London, (Nicolas,) p. 120. The names of those beheaded were John Maddeleye, John Lunday, Thomas Palmere, and Thomas Talbot.

[e] *Read* Rouen.

cardnalle of the Holy Crosse, and asoyllyd the duke of Burgone for the othe that he made un to the kynge of Ynglonde unwyttynge unto the pope, for he had layd sege un to Callys and he faylyd of hys purpose.

xiiij°. A°. Thys yere the towne of Depe was tane by the Armenobis [a] on Halhalon evyn. And the towne of Harflete lost for defaute of good kepynge. And the duke of Burgane a fore sayd layed sege un to Callys the xxix. day of Jule.

xv°. A°. Thys yere sanke a parte of London brygge with two arches. And quene Jane [b] dyde.

xvj°. A°. Thys yere brake owte of the kynges jayle of Newgatte Owyn by the helpe of hys prest, and wondyd hys keper, who had prevyly weddyd qwene Katerne.[c] And also this yere felle downe another parte of London brygge.

xvij°. A°. Thys yere the erle of Warwyke dyde at Roane, the last day of Aprill. And this yere the comyn strompettes that ware takene in London ware raye hoddes. And this yere a bushylle of whette was at forty pence.

xviij°. A°. Thys yere the cardnalle of Wenchester with other lordes came homeward frome Callys to London, that had bene in France to make a pes. And this yere ware dyvers men of Kent drawe and hongyd for tresone agayne the kynge and the church.

And sir John erle of Huntyngtone came thys yere from Guyen in to Ynglond. And this yere the duke of Yorke was made regent of France. And sir Richard Wyche and hys clarke ware burnyd. And this yere was a grete debate arose betwene Fletstrete and the howsys of corte.

xix°. A°. Thys yere was put to deth master Roger Bolyngbroke.[d] And a stryffe in the yelde halle for chesynge of the mayer, by the crafte of the taylors.

a Armeniacs, the forces of the comte of Armagnac.

b *Read* Katharine.

c See the very curious passage on this incident in Chron. of London (Nicolas).

d "A man expert in nygromancy" (Fabyan), and one of the councillors of Alianor Cobham, duchess of Gloucester, as mentioned in the next year.

xx°. A°. Thys yere Alionor Cobhame conspyryd the kynges deth by the concell of master Roger clarke and nigromancer, the wyche Alionore was put by the kynge and hys justys to perpetuall prisone; and on sent Arkynwoldes evyne she went a fote to Powlles in blacke, with a taper in hare hande, lede betwene two knyghttes. And in the same wyse on the morrow she went unto crystcherche.[a]

xxj°. A°. Thys yere the lorde Talbot came in to Ynglond and was made erle of Shrowsbery and amyralle of the see. And sir Christofor Talbot was falsely slayne at Callys.

xxij°. A°. Thys yere the byshoppe of Bathe[b] was made chanceler of Englond and archebychopp of Canterbery. And the lord Fanoppe dyde this yere, and is burryd in hys chappell that he made in the freeres precheres.[c]

xxiij°. A°. Thys yere on Candelmas evyne was gret thunder and tempest, that Powlles stepulle on the sowth-west syde mervelusly was sett a fyer, and the stepull of Kyngstone up Temse brent, and many men slayne. And qwene Margaret was crownyd. And the parlament that yere at Byrry.

xxv°. A°. Thys yere was a fyghtynge in Smythfelde betwene ane armerar of fletstret and his servant for worddes ayenst the kynge wherof hys servant apelyd hym; and the servant slew the master in the felde. And this yere the duke of Gloceter dyde at Byrry in the parlament tyme there. And this yere John Chalons sqwere, sonne of Roberte Chalons knyght of Ynglond, fowth in France with the lorde Boyles brother, and John Chalons slew hym in the felde. And thys yere was juggyd to be drawne, hungyd, but they ware but drawne, Chamberlyn, Myddyltone, Artoys, Herberd, and Nedeham; but whane they ware drawne they had ther pardone all and their lyffes.

xxvj°. A°. Thys yere the kynge made two dukes, of Norfolke and Suffoke. And this yere the watter of the Temse by excesse

[a] The priory at Aldgate.

[b] John Stafford.

[c] Sir John Cornwall, K.G. who had married Elizabeth duchess of Exeter, sister to king Henry IV. His chantry chapel was at the Black friars in London.

of floode the monday in Ester weke came and incresid on the londe unto Populer, and drownyd many howsys and feldes and medowes, and moche of the parich of Stepney, and at Raynham and other places in Essex.

xxvij°. A°. Thys yere was another dere yere, and ane erthqwake.

xxviij°. A°. Thys yere Normandy was lost. And this yere came Jake Cade of Kent, and made hym selfe a captayne with a gret multytude of pepulle unto Blackehethe, and there abode seven dayes contynually unto that the kynge with his lordes that lay that tyme at sent Johns in Smythfelde and in divers placis came rydynge thurgh London toward Grenewich; and thene Jake Cade fledde and removyd fro thens toward Tunbrych, Maydstone, and Senoke. And there hys men beheddyd a sqwere callyd Stanlaw. And in that contre there was sir Humfry Stafford knyght and William Stafford sqwere, with certayne men of armes, slayne. And in that mene tyme came a captayne of Essex with hys men and enterd in to the felde, and that same tyme was Horne the alderman arestyd. And the satterday the iij^{de} day of July the captayne rode thorrow London to Powlles and to Newgate, and soo forthe to Myle ende. And there was be-heddyd one Cromer of Kent and one Baylly of Colchester, and at the standerd in Cheppe was sir Roger Fench be-heddyd, and at the Whyt harte in Southwarke one Hawaydyne of sent Martyns was be-heddyd; and Malpas of London drewe the cheynne of London brygge, and there was a gret battelle made by nyght agaynst the towne, and many men slayne and drownyd. And sarteyn aldermen of London was there slayne, and the prisoneres of the kynges bench and marchelsay delyveryd owte by Jake Cades commandement. And afterward he was slaine in Kent.

xxix°. A°. Thys yere was Gwyene lost, and the erle of Shrowysbery slayne at Burdos.

xxx°. A°. Thys yere the duke of Yorke sette hys felde at Brent hethe in Kent.

xxxj°. A°. Thys yere the lorddes servanttes made a fray at the wrestlynge place.

xxxij°. A°. Thys yere the mayer lefte rydynge to Westmyster, and went be watter.

xxxiij°. A°. Thys yere was a felde at sent Albons betwene the kynge and the duke of Yorke.

xxxv°. A°. Thys yere the lorde Egremond brake owte of Newgate, and had a hors redy and rode a way and one of the jaylers with hym. And in the ende of this same yere came the Frenchmen and other enmyes, and spoylyd and robbyd the good porte of Sandwych, and slewe moche pepulle; for they came sodenly to Sandwych in the mornynge when men ware a bede, and serched every house, and alle the plate, riches, golde, sylver, and othere merchandys and gooddes of valewe they sheppyd it into theire sheppes and went smotly a way with all.

xxxvj°. A°. Thys yere the xxvij. day of November, that tyme was sonday, Pecoke that was byshoppe of Chechester stode at Powlles crosse, wych was apeched of dyvers poynttes of eryses, and there he abjuryd and revokyd them in the prechenynge tyme in the presens of the byshoppe of Cauntorbury, the byshoppe of London, and byshoppe of Durhame, and other prelattes. And also there in the prechenge tyme ware many bokes of eryses of hys makynge, that cost moche gooddes, damnyd and brent be fore hys face. And doctor William Gooddard the elder,[a] that was provinciall of the Greyfreeres, apechyd hym of hys erysys. And this same yere was the ryall syght and wache of men of armes in London that ever was sene, of a gret number of clene ownest men goynge owte of Newgate, and soe up Holborne and downe Chauncery lanne and thorow Fletstret and in at Ludgate and thorow Temstret, and soo to the tower of London, and soe forthe home agayne.

xxxvij°. A°. Thys yere was a felde at Ludlow, and at Blore hethe, and a fraye betwene men of the kynges howse and men of lawe.

[a] His tomb was in the choir of the Grey Friars' church—"venerabilis pater et frater Willelmus Goddard, doctor egregius, et ordinis fratrum minorum in Anglia minister benemeritus; qui obiit 30° die mensis Octobris A° dni 1437." Collectanea Topographica et Genealogica, vol. v. p. 277.

xxxviij°. A°. Thys yere was another felde at sent Albons, and the felde at Northamtone, and at Wakefelde, and at Mortymers crosse, anno M^{l}ccccxvj.

xxxix°. A°. Thys yere was a felde be syde Yorke, and kynge Henry put downe, and the ducke of Yorke eldest sonne toke up one hym the crowne, and was callyd Edwarde the iiijth. And at this felde was slayne xxxij M^{l}. men.

EDWARDUS QUARTUS REX.

P^{io} A°. Thys yere was the erle of Oxenford be-heddyd and other gentylmen.

ij°. A°. Thys yere the towne dech was new cast. And Palmesonday felde. And the towne of Barwyke wanne.

iij°. A°. Thys yere was the sarganttes fest, and the mayer dyned not there, and for be cause that he satt not princypall bothe he and the comyns went a waye at that tyme. And this yere was the battelle of Hexhame felde.

iiij°. A°. Thys yere the qwene was crownyd. And kynge Henry put in to the Towere. And the rose nobyll at x^{s}., the aungell at vj^{s}. viij^{d}.

v°. A°. Thys yere came grete lordes from the londe of Poole and Beame to see thys lond.

vj°. A°. Thys yere a battell in Smythfelde betwene the lorde Scales and the basterd of Burgoyne, and the lorde Scales had the worchyppe of the felde.

vij°. A°. Thys yere was the kynges suster Margaret marryd unto Charles duke of Burgone.

viij°. A°. Thys yere was taken the lorde Harbord and hys brother at Hedgcot felde and both be-heddyd, and the lorde Ryvers and hys sone be-heddyd, and one Stafforde of Soutwyke that was made erle Dennsher be-heddyd also.

ix°. A°. Thys yere at Ester the duke of Clarans and the erle of Warwyke flede into France. And Poynes and Alford be-heddyd.

And at Myhylmas the lordes came agayne into Englond and the kynge flede into Hollonde, and kynge Henry put agayne to the crowne. And the erle of Worceter be-heddyd. And the prince borne. And a blacke sterre. And the battelle of Stamford.

x°. A°. Thys yere the kynge came agayne in to Ynglond in Lent, and dyd a battell at Barnet on Ester day, and there was slayne the erle of Warwyke and hys brother markes Montagu, and kyng Henry put agayne into the tower. And a battelle at Teukysbury there was slayne kynge Henrys sone and many other lordes and knyttes. And the basterd Fauconbryge came from the see with hys retenew, [and] wolde have entered the citte, but he was manly defendyd by the cittezens and many of hys men slayne.

xj°. A°. Thys yere in July was borne Richard the kynges ij^{de} sone, and he was made duke of Yorke.

xij°. A°. Thys yere was ordenyd in every warde a payer of stockes; and that yere fifteen women ware ray hoddes.

xiij°. A°. Thys yere was a fray on sent Peteres evyn betwene the kynges servantes and the wache men of the citte of London.

xiiij°. A°. Thys yere the kynge went in to France ward at Mydsomer, and londyd at Callys with a grete armey, and hys host went to Amias, and there spake with the Frenche kynge and there made pece with owte battelle, and the Frenche kynge heldynge [b] yerly xj M^{l}. li. and soo came home agayne.

xvj°. A°. Thys yere beganne the reparacions of the walles of the citte of London, and the deches abowte new cast.

xvij°. A°. Thys yere the ducke of Clarans was put to dethe. And the terme deferrd from Ester to Myhylmas be cause of the grete pestelens.

xix°. A°. Thys yere the kynges syster duches of Burgone came in to Ynglond to see hare brother. And this yere the kynge taxid sore hys lond.

[a] yielding.

xxj°. A°. Thys yere the kynge made a grete army into Scotland by hys brother the duke of Glocester, in the wyche viage he wane Barwike. And a gret derth of corne.

xxij°. A°. Thys yere desceeid the kynge [xxij day] in Aperlle enterynge in to the xxiij. yere of hys rayne.

RICARDUS TERTIUS REX.

And the two sonnyes of kynge Edward were put to cilence, and the duke of Glocester toke upone hym the crowne in July, wych was the furst yere of hys rayne. And he and hys qwene crownyd on one daye in the same monyth of July.

ij°. A°. Thys yere the duke of Buckyngham was be-heddyd at Salsbery, and is burryd at the Gray freres.[a] And many lordes [and] knygttes with dyvers other flede into France at that tyme.

[a] This is a passage of some interest in relation to a matter which has been enveloped in considerable obscurity. Even some doubt has been entertained with regard to the place of Buckingham's execution, owing to the chronicler Grafton having stated that it was at Shrewsbury, and having been followed in that statement by Holinshed, Echard, and Rapin. This, however, has been entirely set at rest by Mr. Blakeway the historian of that town, and by Mr. Hatcher the historian of Salisbury, who agree that Salisbury was the place. Then, as to the duke's interment, Mr. Hatcher, perhaps encouraged by the triumph of having vindicated this historical incident in favour of his own town, proceeds so far as to say (History of Salisbury, folio, 1843, p. 207): "If the fact of Buckingham's execution at Salisbury be considered as indisputably established, we shall not be guilty of too great a stretch of imagination, in supposing that these were his mutilated remains interred clandestinely, or at least without ceremony, near the spot where he suffered"—referring to the discovery of a headless skeleton beneath the floor of an outhouse near the stone on which Buckingham was traditionally said to have suffered. From a quarter less authoritative than an historian in folio, such a conjecture might, perhaps, be disregarded. It is obvious that during the many generations which have passed since the execution of Buckingham, there might have been many opportunities of concealing in the out-buildings of an inn the remains of some way-laid traveller, or the victim of some ale-house brawl. But, an undue importance having been given to the notion that the skeleton was that of the princely Buckingham, the present passage comes in aid to correct the facility with which Mr. Hatcher yielded to an hypothesis so fanciful. It shows that the duke's body received that attention which the religious orders were always ready to bestow on such occasions, and that it was interred in the church of the Grey Friars

iij°. A°. This yere in August the erle of Richmond with the erle of Pembroke that long hade bene banyshed, came into Ynglond, and the other gentylmen that flede into France, [and] made a felde besyde Leyceter, and the kynge there slayne.

HENRICUS SEPTIMUS REX.

And the erle of Richmond was crownyd kynge, and was callyd Henre the Seventh, the xxx. day of October; and abowte Candelmas marryd kynge Edwardes eldest dougter. And this yere in September dyde Thomas Hylle [the mayor], and for hyme was chosyn William Stocker, and he dyde the third day after and thane was chosyn John Warde, and he occopyed tyll Myhylmas.

P^io^. A°. Thys yere was a gret dethe and hasty, callyd swettyng sykenes. And the crosse in Chepe new made. And a grete taske and a disme grauntyd. And a bushylle of bay salte at iij^s^. iiij^d^.

ij°. A°. Thys yere the qwene was crownyd. And the erle of Lyncolne and the lord Lovell and one Martyn Swarte a stranger all ware slayne in a felde that they made agaynst the kynge at Newarke.

iij°. A°. Thys yere prince Arture was borne at Wenchester. And this yere the kynge went un to Bullen.

iiij°. A°. Thys yere the kynge sent many knyghttes in to Bretayne with the number of vij. M^l^. men to defende the two ladys that ware ayeres to the lond. And the erle of Nortumberlond slayne in the North. And the cape of mayntenans browte from Rome.

at Salisbury. A MS. in the library of the Society of Antiquaries, No. 99, also states the same fact. Another misapprehension has been entertained in connection with this subject, namely, that a monument still existing in the church of Britford, near Salisbury, and engraved in Sir Richard C. Hoare's Hundred of Cawden, was that of the duke of Buckingham. It is unnecessary to repeat here the considerations which decidedly negative that appropriation; but they will be found in the Gentleman's Magazine for June 1836, and in Sir R. C. Hoare's History of Modern Wiltshire, Addenda, p. 61.

v°. A°. Thys yere Cryppylle gate was new made. And Edmond Franke and others put to deth.

vj°. A°. Thys yere sir Robert Chamberlyne lorde be-heddyd. And in June the kynges ij[de] sone was borne at Grynwyche, and namyd Henry. And the condyd at Graschurch begonne and new made.

vij°. A°. Thys yere in September the kynge went to Callys with a grete armé agaynst France, but the pece was made with-owte battelle. And the qwenys moder dicessyd. And the lovers [a] sett up on the yelde halle of London.

viij°. A°. Thys yere was a rysynge of yonge men agaynst the stelyard. And whett at vj[d]. a bushelle.

x°. A°. Thys yere was beheddyd sir William Stanle lorde chamberlyne, sir Robert Ratcleffe, sir Simonde Momforde, and William Daukus;[b] and lorde Fewalter be-heddyd at Callys. And this yere whyt herynge was solde at iij[s]. iiij[d]. the barrelle. And lorde Monforde sone and many others that londyd in the downes to the number of viij. score that came from one Perkyne Warbyke callynge hymselfe kynge Edward sone.

xij°. A°. Thys yere the commons of Cornwall arose to the number of xxx. M[l]., and the lorde Audle cheffe captayne, and one Flammoke and a smythe that was callyd Myhyll Joseffe; and they came to Blackheth and made a felde agaynst the kynge and lost it. The captayns tane and put to excecucione. Thys felde was in June on sent Bothols day. And in August after one Perkyne Warbyke, callyng [c] hym-selfe the second sone of kynge Edwarde the iiij[th], londyd in Cornewalle; and he was persewyd of sartayne lordes, but he flede to Bewdley senttuary, and by apoyntment came to the kynge, and so remaynyd followynge the corte.

xiij°. A°. Thys yere in December the wedercoke, crosse, and the bowle of Powlles stepulle was tane downe and all newe made, and in May after solemply hallowyd and sett up agayne. And this same yere in August was the second provinciall chapter of the Freer

[a] louvres. [b] *Read* Dawbeney. [c] *MS.* callyd.

minores in London. And there beganne the Observanttes, and came with the kynges letters and commandment for sertayne placis, and so beganne with Newcastelle, Cauntorbery, and Sowthamtone.

And the kynges loggyne at Shene burnyd. Perkyn Warbyke sett on a skaffold in Chepe.

xiiij°. A°. Thys yere the xxij. daye of February was borne at Grenwyche the third sone of kynge Henry the Seventh, namyd Edmonde duke of Somerset.

xv°. A°. Thys yere in November Perkyne Warbyke was convicte of tresone and draune from the tower of London to Tyborne, and there hongyd and be-heddyd; and the same tyme was juggyd to dye for tresone the erle of Warwyke sone to the duke of Clarans be fore rehersyd, wyche erle had bene kepte in the tower from the age of xj. yere un to the ende of xiiij. yere after, and the xxviijth. day of November was beheddyd at the towre hyll. And the same daye was grete flooddes, wynddes, thunder, lytnynges, wyche dyd moche harme and hurte in dyvers placys and countres in Ynglonde.

And the viij. daye of May nexte after the kynge and the qwene went to Callys, and thether came the duke of Burgone and spake with the kynge [a] in sent Peters church withowte the towne the space of seven oweres with moche honor and solas, and so departyd. And the xiiij. day of June after the kynge and qwene came home agayne. Thys was in the yere of our Lord xv C.
And the same monyth in December descessid the kynges thurde sonne Edmonde, and was burryd at Westminster. And the same yere dyde the archbyshoppe of Yorke,[b] the byshoppe of Norwyche,[c] and the byshoppe of Elye.[d] And in September followynge dyscessyd the the byshoppe of Cauntorbery, Morton, cardnalle and chaunceler of Ynglond. And this yere was brent a palmer. And a grete pestelens thorrow all Ynglonde and a grete d[earth.]

xvj°. A°. Thys yere the kynge byldyd new hys maner of Shene, and changed the name and namyd it Richemonde, and he byldyd new

[a] See a full narrative of this interview in the Appendix to the Chronicle of Calais, p. 49.

[b] Thomas Scott, alias Rotherham.

[c] Thomas Jane, or Jaun.

[d] John Alcock.

his place called Baynystcastell[a] in London, and repayryd hys place at Grenewyche, with moche newe byldynge there and in dyvers places.

xvij°. A°. Thys yere was send in to Ynglonde the kynge of Spaynyes thurde daughter, namyd Kateryne, to be marryd to the prince Arture, and she londyd at Plummothe the viij. day of October, and res[eved] in to lond in the most ryall wyse the xij. day of November than fryday. And the sonday followynge maryd at sent Powlles churche. And a halpas made of tymber from the west dore to the qwere dore of twelve foote brode and four fotte of hyghte. And in the myddes of the same marryd. And the fest holden in the byshoppe of Londones palles. And the day of hare reseving in to lond was made many reche pagenttes; furst at the bregge, at the condyd in Graschestret, the condet in Cornelle, standàrde in Cheppe, the crosse new gylted, at the lyttyll condyd, and at Powlles west dore, ronnynge wyne, rede claret and wythe, and alle the day of the marrage. And at the same maryge the kynge made fifty-seven knyghttes. And the iij[de] day after alle the corte removyd unto Westmyster by watter. And the mayer wyth alle the crafttes wyth them in barges, with trompettes, shalmes, and taberttes in the best maner; and there the kynge helde ryall justes, turnayes, and bankettes six dayes after. And thene returnyd to Rychemonde. And the same daye ther the mayer helde hys fest at the yelde halle.

And the same yere in November came to the kynge a nobyll imbassator owte of Scotland for to trete of maryage betwene the Scottyche kynge and our kynges eldest dowgter namyd Margarete, wyche was acordyd on sent Powlles evyn the conversion. And the second sonday of lent[b] after was sir Edmonde de la Poole was pronuncyd acursed opynly wyth boke, belle, and candell, at Powlles crose at the sermonde before none. And in Ester weke nexte after dyscecyd the prince Arture at Ludlow, and burryd at Worceter. And the deche from the Temse to Holborne brygge new cast. And this yere the Gray freeres changed their abbyttes in to whytte gray apone sent Georges day, thene beynge sattorday the

[a] Baynard's Castle.

[b] Fabyan mentions this "upon the *first* sonday of Lent" in the next year.

prime in the yere of our lorde M[l]ccccij.[a] And sir James Tyrryll and sir John Wyndham be-hedyd.[b] Thys yere the qwene Elizabeth dyde[c] at the towre, and burryd at Westmyster. Item this yere a gret imbassetor came from the kynge of Romans. And the Gray freeres chaungyd their habbetts from London rossette unto whytt gray.[d]

xviij°. A°. Thys yere was the gret jubele at Powlles.

xix°. A°. Thys yere Margarete that was the kynges daughter was marryd unto the kynge of Scottes. And that same yere in March was a grete frost and snowe, and many grete fyeres in London in dyvers places, as at the brigge, Austyn freeres, sent Martyns grante,[e] and Buttoll w[harf?] And a gret fray in Cheppe, [wherein] lordes and knyttes toke partes.

xxj°. A°. Thys yere the xv. day of January at twelve of cloke at none rose soche a tempest of wynde tyll it was twelve at mydnyth, that it blew downe tres and tyles of howsys, and that same nyght it blewe downe the weddercoke of Powlles stepulle the lengthe of the ende of Powlles church unto the syne of the blacke egylle; at that tyme was lowe howses of bokebynderes wher nowe is the scole of Powles. And that same nyght was the duke of Burgone that was callyd Phyllype with hys lady and many shepes of hys, the wyche intendyd to a gone into Spayne to a bene crownyd kynge, but by tempest ware drevyne to Porchemoth havyne, and soo the kynge send many of the nobyll lordes and states of the realme both speri-tuall and temporall to reseve hym and all hys pepull, and soo browte them to London; and there the kynge nobylly reseved them and made them grete chere and soo departyd them home agayne. And that same yere at that tyme was soch a sore snowe and a frost that men myght goo with carttes over the Temse and horse, and it lastyd

[a] "Also aboute thys tyme the Gray fryers were compelled to take theyr old habit russet as the shepe doth dye it."—Fabyan.

[b] On the vj. day of May on Tower hill, says Fabyan: they were partisans of Sir Ed-mund de la Pole.

[c] On the 11th Feb. 1502-3.

[d] The four last lines are an addition to the original MS.; whence occurs this repetition.

[e] St. Martin's le Grand. Fabyan gives the respective dates of these fires.

tylle after candelmas. And then it was agreed betwene the kynge and the duke of Burgone that Edmond de la Poole shulde be send home agayne, and so he was.

xxij°. A°. This yere was chosyn [sheriff] by the citte one Jonson a goldesmythe, and he made hys fest; but within iij. dayes he was dyschargyd at the commandment of the kynge, and William Fitzwilliam chosyn, and so kepte owte alle the hole yere, and the other toke soche a thowthe that he dyde. Item the bakeres howse in Warwyke lane burnyd. And twelve herynges a j^{d}. And a gally burnyd at Hamton.

xxiij°. A°. Thys yere was many aldermen put in to the tower, and sir William Capell put to warde in the shreffes howse. And this yere the mayer was reseved with procession on sent Frances daye with the aldermen as founders,[a] and soo contynewyd long after.

And the lady Mary the kynges dowter made sewre to the kynge of Castelle.

xxiiij°. A°. Thys yere the xxij. day of Aprill dyde kynge Henry the vijth at Richemonde, and browth to London over the brygge and soo to Powlles the furst nyght, and the nexte day to Westmyster nobylly and there buryd.

HENRICUS OCTAVUS REX.

And the mydsomer day followynge was his sonne crownyd Henry the viijth at Westmyster, and hys qwene Kateryne that was hys brothers wyffe prince Artore. Thys yere was Emsone and Dodle be-heddyd at Towre hyll. And four persons sett on the pyllory for falls qwestmongeres.

iiij°. A°. Thys yere the kynge went in to France, and the carreke and the Regent byrnte. And this yere was the Scottych felde, and the kynge tane and slayne, and browte to Shene.

vj°. A°. Thys yere was a gret deth at the Menerys, that there dyde xxvij. of the nonnes.

[a] At the Grey Friars.

viij°. A°. Thys yere was yell May day, that yong men and prentes of London rose in the nyght, and wolde have had James Mottas ane owte-landych mane and wölde have slayne hym, but he hyde hym in hys gotters in hys howse; and from thense they wente un to sent Martyns, and there spoyled the shomakers shoppes of shone; and thane rose the mayer and shreffes and wolde have cessyd them, but they cowde not. And then rose the erle of Surre, and he wolde have spoyled them. And iiij. or v. dayes after the corte kepte the citte in harnes with divers lordes, and at the last there ware dyvers of them hongyd within the citte on gallos, as at sent Martyns gatte at Ludgate, at Algate, Bysshoppes gate, Doggate, sent Manguns, Ledynhall, in the Powltre, and at the stondert in Cheppe; and there was hongyd and qwarterd one Lyncon; and another gallows at Newgate. And within shorte space the kynge satte in Westmyster halle, and there was commandyd the citte to come in their clothynge, and the rest of them that was pardent to come with halters abowte their neckes and to aske pardone, and soo a generall pardone was gevyne unto theme alle that came that tyme.

xij°. A°. Thys yere was the duke of Buckynghame be-heddyd at the towre hylle, and burryd at the Austynfreeres. And the owyns[a] made at the bryge howse.

xiij°. A°. Thys yere the emperor Charles came in to Ynglond and soo to London, and there was honorabullie resevyd with many pagenttes, as on the brygge, in Graschestret, Ledynhalle, the condet in Cornell, at Stockes, at the gret condet in Chepe, at the standerd, the crosse new gylte, at the lyttell condet, and Powlles church dore; and soe to Bryddewell, wych was new made and gylte agenst hys comynge.

And this yere was a man soddyne in a cautherne[b] in Smythfelde, and lett up and downe dyvers tymes tyll he was dede, for because he wold a poyssynd dyvers persons.

xiiij°. A°. Thys yere the kynge of Denmarke and hys qwene was drevyn oute of their londe for cruelnes that he dyd unto hys

[a] ovens. [b] Boiled in a caldron.

perys and hys pepull in hys realme, and harde masse in Powlles church [a] with hys qwene. And from thens went unto Westmyster.

And this yere thys mayer [b] beganne the furst fest that the mayer shuld dyne on sent Frances day in the Grayfreeres.

And this yere in feverelle the xx^{ti}. day was the lady Alys Hungrford was lede from the tower un to Holborne and there put into a carte at the church-yard with one of her servanttes, and so caryed unto Tyborne, and there both hongyd,[c] and she burryd at the Greyfreeres in the nether end of the myddes of the church on the north syde.

And the parlament beganne at the Black freeres, where every man was sworn what he was worth and to paye to the kynge.

xv°. A°. Thys yere was moch adoo for the mayer, for master Gorge Monop was chosyne, but he wolde not take it aponne hym. And then on Simone and Judes evyne master Baldere toke it on hym.

And this yere was drawne and hongyd and quarterd at Tyborne for tresone Frances, Antony, and Pekerynge, for thei intendyd to a made an insurrexsion with in the londe at Coventre.

And here the erle of Angwych [d] came in to Ynglond.

xvj°. A°. Thys yere the kyng and the cardnall Wolsey the ixth. day of Marche *intendyd to a* come and to see the Grayfreeres *but the ware lett tyll* . . .[e] And the xvj. day of January, before the byshoppe of sent Asse doctor Standych and doctor Ally and other offeceres belongynge unto the sayd legate dyd begynne their visitacion at the Observanttes at Grenwych, and then was departyd many of them unto other placys; but agayne that day that the byshoppe of sent Asse with

[a] "Christierne king of Denmark came into Englande in June." Fabyan.

[b] John Munden, goldsmith.

[c] This lady's crime was that of having murdered her husband, as Stowe seems to have gathered from some other authority, though his passage on this subject is mainly from the present chronicle. The parties have not hitherto been identified; but see a note in the Addenda to the present volume.

[d] Archibald Douglas earl of Angus the husband of Margaret queen dowager of Scotland, sister to king Henry. He came into England out of France.

[e] The words in Italic are struck through.

his compeny shulde come agayne, many of them were come home agayne, or elles they had bene put owte at that tyme; and one of that owse John Forrest was comandyd to preche at Powlles crosse the sonday after, and there pronuncid them all acurst that wente owte of the place; and thene some of theme came home, and ware put in the porteres warde in the cardnalles place. And amonge all was one lay brother William Renscrofte was send un to the Gray freeres in London to prisone and was there longe, and at the last submyttyd hymselfe and was asoyled of the sayd byshoppe by the auctoryte of the cardnall, and soe delyverd home agayne.

Also that day that the kynge came owte of hys chamber to come to the Gray freeres tydynges was browte hym that the Frenche kynge was tane by the duke of Burgone. Also there was gevyne commandement unto the mayer that that nyght that there shulde be a gret bonfyer at Powlles churche dore, and there to be sett a hoggys hed of rede and another of claret for the pepulle to drynke that wolde for the good tydynges. And the second day after was satterday at nyght was a grete wache thorrow all the citte as it is wonte to be at mydsomer, and in every stret a bone fyer. And the sonday after, wyche was the second of lent, the kynge, qwene, and princes,[a] with all other stattes both spirituall and temporall, came to Powlles, and there was songe Te Deum. And after masse the legate gave hys benediccion to all that was in the churche, clene lyffe clene remission.

Also the thursday at nyght, after that Bowe bell was ronge, a pele was comandyd to be ronge in every parish church in London for sewer worde and tydynges that Richard de la Pole was slayne,[b] and many of the nobyll stattes of France there to the number of xxx M^{l}.

And this same yere was dyvers of the Austyne freeres put in the tower of London for a freer that dyde in prisone amonge them.

And on sent Mathie daye after was a grete generall procescion

[a] Princess (Mary). [b] At the battle of Pavia.

with every places of relegione in their best coppis, clarkes and prestes, and so went from Pawlles uppe to Ledyne hall, and downe Grascherch and to sent Mangylles, and all Temstrete; and uppe at Doggate, and uppe Watlyngstrete, and soo to Pawlles west dore, there the cardnalle with dyvers byshoppes and abbottes in their mytteres; and soo came in to Pawlles to the hye autter, and there sange Te Deum for the sewer tydynges that was come of this beforesayd.

And a bushylle of baye salte solde for iiij s. viij d.

xvij°. A°. Thys yere beganne the cardnalle Wolsey to enter hys visitacione amonge the iiij. cl . . . and on Alsolne day doctor Allyn beganne in the Gray freeres at afternone.

And in thys yere begane the golde to ryse, as the angell nobyll at vij s. and in November after it was made vij s. vj d.; and here begane a derth of corne.

xviij°. A°. Thys yere was moch a doo in the yelde-halle for the mayer, for the comyns wold not have had Semer, for be cause of yell May day.[a] And also whane the shereffe shulde be chosyn for the comyns they chose *(blank)*, but he wold not take it, and soo it stode voyed tyll it was Myhylmas daye, and then master Lambert toke it.

Also this same yere doctor Barnes[b] the Austyne freer, two Esterlynges, and two other men shulde a stonde at Powlles crosse at the sermonde with faggottes and tapers, but for because of rayne they stode on the hye scaffolde within the church, and the byshoppe of Rochester Fycher dyd preche; this was the xvj. day of February, and then Barnes was delyveryd home to prisone, but he brake aways from them and went beyend see unto Luter.

And the vj. day of October was a gret rayne all the nyght and all the daye unto vj. a cloke at nyghte, and then was gret lytnynge and thunder and haylle.

And this yere was a gret derth in London for brede, that dyvers persons both men and women ware hurte at the carttes. And moch

[a] Thomas Semer had been sheriff when the riot occurred recorded in p. 30.

[b] Robert Barnes, prior of St. Augustine's at Cambridge, afterwards burnt in 1540.

wette and rye was provyded for in London in dyvers howses for the citte.[a]

And this yere the pope was tane prisoner by the emperor, and dyvers cardnalles, and afterward was ransomyd un to the emperor.

The xxiiij. day of October after was a gret generall procession agayne in their coppis, and at Powlles west dore mett the cardnalle with dyvers byshoppes, abbottes, and priors, in their mytters agayne.

And thys yere the cardnalle went in to France for to make a lege betwene the kynge and us; and this yere in October after the grand master of France[b] came to London.

xix°. A°. Thys yere was noo wache on Mydsomer nyght. And also this yere was gret derth for brede.

xx°. A°. This yere was a prisoner brake from the halle at Newgate whan the cecions was done, that was browte downe in a basket and brake thorow the pepull and went unto the Grayfreeres, and there was vij. dayes. And at the last the shreffes came and spoke with hym in the church, and, for because he wolde not abjure and aske a crowner, with gret violens of them and their offecers toke him owte of the churche, and soo the churche was shott in from monday unto thursday, and the servys and masse sayd and songe in the fratter; and that day the bushoppe of sent Asse[c] browte the sacrament solemply downe with procession, and soo the powre prisoner contineywd in prisone, for they sowte all the wayes that they cowde but the lawe wolde not serve them to honge hym, and at the last was delyvered and put at lyberte.

Also this same yere John Scotte, that was one of the kynges playeres, was put in Newgate for rebukynge of the shreffes, and was there a sennet, and at the last was ledde betwene two of the offecers from Newgate thorrow London and soe to Newgat agayne, and then was delyveryd home to hys howse; but he toke soch a thowte that he dyde, for he went in hys shurte.

[a] The people appear to have been injured when crowding and pressing round the carts laden with corn as they stood in the market. To prevent such accidents in future the carts were unladen and the corn deposited for sale in shops.

[b] The Maréchal de Montmorency. See Cavendish's Wolsey, Singer's Ed. p. 188.

[c] Henry Standish.

And this yere in June two legattes satt at the Blacke freeres for the kynges marryge; and in October the cardnalle was deprived of the chanslercheppe.

xxj°. A°. Thys yere at mydsomer was a goodly wache and two goodly pagenttes in Cheppe-syde at Soper lane ende.

And this yere was the emperor crowned at Bonony.

xxij°. A°. Thys yere was moche a doo for chesynge of the shreffe; the comyns wolde have had Amadas, but he wolde not take it; and at the last on Myhylmas evyn was chosyn Richard Choppyne chandler, and there by and by toke his hothe in the yelde halle and soo went to Westmyster.

And this yere was gret wyndes and fluddes that dyde moch harme both a thys syde the see and beyende the see.

The xj. day of May the challons of Esyngspettylle[a] was put owte.

Also this yere was a coke boylyd in a cauderne in Smythfeld for he wolde a powsynd the byshoppe of Rochester Fycher with dyvers of hys servanttes,[b] and he was lockyd in a chayne and pullyd up and downe with a gybbyt at dyvers tymes tyll he was dede.

And this yere dyde the cardnalle Wolsey on sent Andrewys evyn, and byrryd at Lecetter.

xxiij°. A°. This yere was a chauntery prest of sent Andrewys at Baynyscastell the vth day of July was hongyd at Towre hylle, and drawne from Newgatt, for cleppyng of golde.

And also this yere was William Baynard a man of lawe and too mo with hym, burnyd in Smythfelde for errysee, in May.

And this yere was the challons of Crystes church put owte of there place[c] unto dyvers other places, and the place gevyn un to the lorde chauncelor Thomas Audle.

And this yere was a purser[d] at sent Martyns gate burnyd in Smythfelde for eryssye.

Also the sacrament at sent Buttelles at Aldersgate on Good fryday in the mornynge was stolen oute at the est wyndow, and iij. osttes

[a] The Augustinian canons of Elsyng spital. [b] See Additional Notes.

[c] The priory of Christ's Church within Aldgate; see note in p. 61. [d] A purse-maker.

wrappyd in a rede cloth, and a woman browte it unto the porter of the Grayfreeres, and she tane and browte unto the shreffe Richard Grasshame, and she send unto the cownter, and was there alle Ester daye tyll none, and then delyveryd. And the monday after Lowesonday the curet with all the parich and solempnite sette the osttes home with soleme procession, by the commandment of the byshoppe of London, thene beynge doctor John Stokesley.

And this yere the kynge with lady Anne Bullene went to Callys the ix. day of October, and there spake with the Frenche kynge.

xxiiij°. A°. Thys yere in Lent [1533] dyde Nicolas Pynsone [sheriff], and for hym was chosyn John Martyne bocher; and the xvj. day before Myhylmas he dyde, and for hym was chosyn John Preist grocer.

And this yere was burnyd in Smythfelde, Freth and another with hym, for gret errysy.

And this yere was the coronacion of qwene Anne. The xxix^{ti}. day of May she was browte be watter from Grenwyche un to the tower with barges, the mayer, aldermen, and the craffttes, as the mayer dothe to Westmester whan he takys hys othe; and the satterday after, that was Wytson evyn, came from the tower thorow London; pagenttes as at Gracechurch, at Ledynehalle, the condet in Cornehylle, the gret condet in Cheppe, the standert new payntyd, and the wayttes playnge there, the crosse new burnechyd, the lyttyll condet, and at Powlles gatte, and soo to Whytt halle at Westmyster that some tyme was the byshoppe of Yorkes place, and soo agayne that tyme was new made. And a tylte to just with grete posttes and vanes of the kynges armes and hares,[a] with their conysanttes payntyd and gylte, and with stoneworke up to the raylles, the wych was wrotte[b] on Assencion day in the mornynge. And on Wytsonsonday, which was the xxxj. of May, was the coronacion in Westmyster church; and soo came crownyd from thens to Westmyster halle, and there dynyd, and at that tyme was many knyghttes made.

[a] her's. [b] wrought.

And this yere dyde the Frenche qwene, wyffe un to the duke of Suffoke, Mary that was dowter to Henry the vij.

xxv°. A°. Thys yere the xxiij. day of November [1533] prechyd at Powlles crosse the byshoppe of Bangure electe doctor Capun,[a] and there stode before hym on a skaffolde doctor Bockynge and another monke[b] of the same howse of Crystes church of Cantorbery, the parsone[c] of Aldermary gelde, and ij. Observanttes of Cantorbery,[d] and the holy mayde of Kent[e]; and from thens they went unto the tower of London agayne, and moche pepull both at the crosse and thorrow alle the streetes of London, unto the tower. From thens they went to Cauntorbery, and there dyd pennans also.

And this yere was hongyd at the Wyllow by the Temse syde Woolfe and hys wyffe, for kyllynge of two Lumberttes[f] in a bote on the Temse.

And this yere was the byshoppe of Rome('s) powre pu[t down, and] a pes concludyd with Scotlond that lastyd but a wy[le.]

Thys yere was the mayde of Kent with the monkes, freeres, and the parsone of Aldermary, draune to Tyborne, and there hongyd and heddyd the v. day of May [1534], and the monkes burryt at the Blacke freeres, the Observanttes, with the holy mayde at the Gray freeres; and the parsone at hys church Aldermary.

xxvj°. A°. And this yere the xx[ti]. day of November the lorde amrelle of France[g] came into Ynglond, and was reseved into London with gret solempnyte of the mayer, aldermen, and crafftes of the same, in Chepesyde.

Also the same yere the iij. day of May [1535] was Holy-rode day, and then was draune from the tower unto Tyborne the iij. priors of

[a] John Salcot, alias Capon, late abbot of Hyde by Winchester.

[b] Edward Bocking and Richard Dering.

[c] Henry Gold, M.A. Rector of St. Mary Aldermary, Dec. 10, 1526, and Vicar of Hayes, Middlesex, Dec. 23, 1529.

[d] Hugh Rich, warden of the friars Observants, and Richard Risby.

[e] Elizabeth Barton.

[f] "Twoo marchauntes straungers." Fabyan.

[g] Philip de Chabot comte de Neublanche, K.G.; see Chron. of Calais, p. 45.

the Charterhowses,[a] and there hongyd, heddyd, and qwarterd; and one of the qwarters of the prior's harmes was sett up at the gatte in to Aldersgate stret. And within short whylle after iiij. monkes moo of the sayd howse, as Exmew, Nitygate, with ij. others,[b] ware drawne from the tower to Tyborne, and there hongyd, heddyd, and qwarterd, and their qwarteres sett upp.

Also this yere the xxij. day of July was the byshoppe of Rochester John Fycher beheddyd at Towre hyll, and burryd in the churchyerd of Barkyne by the northe dore. And the xxvj. day of the same month was beheddyd at Towre hyll sir Thomas More some tyme chaunsler of Ynglond, and then was tane up the byshoppe agayne and both of them burryd within the tower.

And that same yere beganne the new testament in Englych.

And this yere dyde the erle of Kyldare in the tower.

And this yere was grantyd unto the kynge the tenthes and furst fruttes both spirituall and temporall.

xxvij°. A°. Thys yere the furst day of Maye [1536] was tane and arestyd of tresone the qwene Anne, lorde Rochford hare brother, master Norres, master West, master Breertone, and one Markes, at Grenewyche, and browte unto the tower. And the xiij. daye after they went unto Westmyster to have their jugment, alle save only the qwene and lorde Rocheford, for they had their jugment within the tower the xv. day of May with the lordes of the realme; and the xvj. of their qwest with the lorde mayer, aldermen, and viij. of every hede craft of London. And the xvij. day of May lorde Rocheforde with alle the rest was beheddyd[c] at Towre hyll, and their heddes sett up one London brygge, and their bodys burryd within the tower. And the xix. day of the same was the qwene Anne[d] beheddyd within the tower, and there burryd.

And in September after was a rysynge in Lyngcolshere of the comons for taske and talenge of ane abbé there, by the menys of

[a] London, Beauvale, and Hexham.

[b] Holinshed names only three, Exmew, Middlemore, and Nudigate.

[c] See the Chronicle of Calais, p. 46.

[d] Vide ibid. p. 47.

lorde Darcy, lorde Husey, sir Robert Constabull, and Roberte Aske. And the vij. day of October the duke of Norffoke and the duke of Suffoke went thether and pacified them; and then beganne Yorkechere to ryse, and they pacifyed them the xxix. day of October. And the kynges grace sent a letter to the mayer and citte of London and gave them thanckes for the paynnes and costtes of sendynge of two hundred and fyfty men the xxxj. day of October.

xxviij°. A°. Thys yere one Robert Pakengtone, mercer, was slayne with a gone the xvij. day of November in a mornyng by the gret condet in Chepe, and then was made a proclemacione by the mayer if anny man canne tell tydynges how he myght be knowyne he shuld have a gret rewarde for hys labor.[a]

Also the iij[de] day of February [1537] the lorde Garrad with hys five unkelles of Ireland—these ware their names, Thomas lorde Fytzgarrard, sir James Fytzgarrard, sir John Fytzgarrard, sir Richard Fytzgarrard lord of sent Ines in Ireland,[b] sir Oliver[c] Fytzgarrard, and sir Watter Fytzgarrard—ware draune from the tower un to Tyborne, and there alle hongyd and heddyd and qwarterd, save the lorde Thomas, for he was but hongyd and heddyd and hys boddy buryd at the Crost Freeres in the qwere, and the qwarteres with their heddes set up abowte the citte.

Also this yere beganne the Corte of Augementacion in Westmyster above by sent Stephens, the wych was now made for the Augmentacion corte, wher as mr. Rich[d] was made chaunceler.

Also the xix. day of Februarij was hongyd at Tyborne x. women and iij. men.

Also this yere in the begynnynge of Lent it was proclamyd and decreed[e] by the kynge and hys concell, that the pepulle shulde ette whytte mettes, and soo dyvers dyde.

[a] The murderer was discovered some years after: see Stowe's Chronicle.

[b] In the genealogy of the FitzGeralds, in Lodge's Peerage of Ireland, by Archdall, 1779, i. 88, sir James FitzGerald of Leixlip, and sir John, are both described as knights of Rhodes, of the order of St. John of Jerusalem; but their brother Richard is not so styled.

[c] Holdner *in MS.*

[d] Richard Rich, afterwards lord high chancellor.

[e] degrees *in MS.*

Also the xiij. day of March sir Frances Bygotte[a] was browte owte of the Northe to the tower thorrow Smythfelde and in at Newgat, rydynge soo thorrow Chepe-syde and soo to the tower, and sir Raffe Elderker ledynge hym by the hond with that he was bounde with alle.

Also this yere the xxv. day of March the Lyncolnechere men that was with bishoppe Makerell was browte owte of Newgate un to the yelde-halle in roppys, and there had their jugment to be draune, hongyd, and heddyd and qwarterd, and soo was the xxix. of March after, the wych was on Maundy thursdaye, and all their qwarters with their heddes was burryd at Pardone church yerde in the frary.[b]

Also the xiiij. day of May was browte from the tower to Westmyster the lorde Darcy and lorde Hussy, and there were condemnide to deth, but they [c] ware had in to the North and there sufferd with Aske.

Also the xvj. day of the same monyth was browte from the towre un to the yelde-halle sir Roberte Constabull and lady Bowmer, but they ware carryd from the yelde-halle unto Westmyster with alle the rest, and there had their jugement. And the xxv. daye of the same monyth was draune from the tower of London un to Tyborne sir John Bowmer knyght, sir Stephen Hamertone knyght, master Nicolas Tempest sqwyere, William Thurston abbot of Fowntens and bachelar of devinite, doctor John Pekerynge prior of the Blacke freeres in Yorke, sir James Pekerelle challon (canon) and doctor of devinite. And after sir John Bowmer [and] sir Stephen Hamertone ware but hongyd and heddyd, and alle the resydew ware bothe hongyd, heddyd and qwarterd. And at that tyme was draune from the tower after, the lady Margarete Bowmer wyffe unto sir John

[a] One of the Northern rebels; who had headed an attack upon the town of Hull.

[b] There was a Pardon churchyard on the north side of St. Paul's cathedral; but this was another near the Charter house, which was used for felons and suicides, and "the priory cart" used for carrying them, belonging to the hospital of St. John at Clerkenwell, which had the privilege of sanctuary, is particularly described by Stowe.

[c] Lord Darcy was beheaded on Tower hill, as subsequently stated; lord Hussey was executed at Lincoln; sir Robert Constable at Hull; and Robert Aske at York.

Bowmer, and he made hare hys wyffe, but she was the wyffe of one Cheyny, for he solde hare un to sir Bowmer; and she was drawne whan she came to Newgate into Smythfelde, and there burnyd the same fore-none. And that same daye at Tyborne was a yonge freere of the Blacke freeres bryngynge up, and for be cause he desyryd the harte of hym that browte hym up, to have it and to burn yt, the shreffe send hym to Newgate and there was a seneyt or more.

Also the ij. daye of June was drawne from the tower of London to Tyborne sir Thomas Percy, sir Frances Byggot, George Lumley eyer to the lorde Lumley, William Woodde prior of Byrlyngtone, Adame Sedbarre abbott of Jarvys, and there ware hongyd, heddyd, and qwarterd, save sir Thomas Percy for he was but heddyd and was burryd at the Crose Freeres, and the qwarters of alle the resydew was burryd at the Gray Freeres in the clowster on the North syde in the pamet.[a] And the xxvi[j?] day of June was hade in to the North to be hongyd and heddyd lorde Husey, sir Robert Constabulle, and Aske, and there sufferde as they ware wordy.

Also the xx. day of June the lorde Darcy was be-heddyd at Towre-hyll, and burryd within the tower.

Also this yere the xij. day of October was borne the prince Edward at Hamton corte, the xxix. yere of kynge Henry the viij.

xxix°. A°. Thys yere the good qwene Jane dessecid the xxiij. day of October at Rechemond, and all the corte had them blacke gownes, and she was burryd at Wynsor the viij. day of November.

Also this yere the xxv. day of February [1538] was drawne from the towere to Tyborne, Henry Harford gentleman and Thomas Hever merchand, and there hongyd and qwarterd for tresone.

Also this yere was made an acte of parliament that no lorde, knyght, sqwier, gentleman, nor yeoman servynge-man shulde dys-obey ony offecer, constabull, bayle, or ony offecer within the citte of London as sargant or yeman, for to drawe any wepone to anny man, oppon payne of deth, or castynge of anny foyne.

[a] pavement?

Also this same yere the xxij. day of May was burnyd in Smythfelde freer John Forrest of Grenewyche, and a rode that came owte of Wallys callyd Delvergaddar.[a]

Also the vij. day of August was put to deth Willyam Conysby gentleman.[b]

And the ij. day of September was put to deth master Clefforde.[c]

And the furst sonday of September was hongyd at Clarkenwell at the wrestlynge place the hongman that was before, and ij. with hym, for stelynge in Bartylmew fayer.

xxx°. A°. Thys yere the xxij. day of November was one Lambert, other wysse callyd Nicolas,[d] was burnyd in Smythfelde for gret eryse.

And the xxix. of November was burnyd in Smythfelde John Mattessey a Docheman, Peter Franke and hys wyffe, for erryse.

And this yere in December was beheddyd at the Towre-hyll lorde Henry markes of Exceter, lorde Henry Montegew,[e] and sir Edward Nevelle.

Also this yere was alle the placys of relygione within the citte of London subprest in November.

Also this yere the xxiij. day of December was burnyd in Smythfelde Richard Turner wever, and Peter Florens bocher.

Also the iij. day of March [1539] was be-heddyd at Towre-hyll sir Nicolas Carrow.

And the viij. day of May was the gret muster in London, that all London musterd in harnes, morys pykes, bowses,[f] hand gons, and whytt cottes, with the mayer, shreffes, and dyvers aldermen.

[a] The shrine of Darvel Gadarn was at Llandervel, co. Merioneth. On the destruction of the image see Wright's Letters on the Suppression of Monasteries, pp. 189, 208; Ellis's Letters, Third Series, letter 330; Ellis's Brand, vol. i. p. 202, edit. 1841.

[b] Stowe says, Edmond Conesby one of the grooms of the king's chamber for counterfeiting the king's seal manual.

[c] Edward Clifford gentleman for counterfeiting the king's privy signet.—Stowe.

[d] Nicholson in Stowe.

[e] Henry Pole viscount Montacute.

[f] harquebus.

Also the ix. day of July was be-heddyd at Towre-hyll master Foskew[a] and master Dyngle[b] knyghttes; and that same day was drawne to Tyborne ij. of their servanttes and ther hongyd and qwarterd for tresone.

xxxj°. A°. Thys yere the xxvij. day of December came in lady Anne of Cleffe in to Ynglond, and the third day of January came to Grenwych, un to the kynges grace, and there was marryd unto the kynges grace with grete solempnyte, with the mayer, aldermen, and xij. crafftes, every one vj.,[d] and theys rode, and all the rest of the crafftes went in their barges with all their best araye as the mayer is wont to goo to Westmyster. And thene beganne alle the gentylwomen of Yngland to were Frenche whooddes with bellementtes[c] of golde.

Also this same yere the xvj. day of March [1540] was one Gomer and iij. vacabundes with him draune, hongyd, and qwarterd for cleppynge of golde, at Tyborne.

Also this same yere at sent Mary spettell, the iij. dayes in Ester weke, preched the vicar of Stepney one Jerome;[e] doctor Barnes[f] the ij[de] daye; and the iij[de] Garrard[g] parsone of Honylane, and there recantyd and askyd the pepulle foryefnes for that they had preched before contrary to the lawe of God. And doctor Barnes, that was the Austyn freer, askyd there the byshoppe of Wenchester foryefnes opynly, and prayd hym yf he wolde foryeffe hym that he wolde make some tokyne and holde up hys honde.

And the x. day of June was arestyd and had unto the tower lorde Thomas Cromewell erle of Essex for grete tresone; and the xxviij. day of July was he and lorde Walter Hungerforthe be-heddyd at

[a] Sir Adrian Fortescue. [b] Sir Thomas Dingley, knight of St. John's.

[c] Habiliments or "biliments," as we find them constantly written, were the jewelled fronts of the ladies' head-dresses, as we see them in the portraits of queen Anne Boleyne, &c. These two lines are added in a contemporary hand.

[d] Six of each of the twelve principal city companies.

[e] William Hierome, or Jerome, instituted to the vicarage of Stepney in 1537.

[f] Robert Barnes, before mentioned in p. 33.

[g] Thomas Garrard, instituted to the rectory of Allhallows, Honey-lane, in 1537.

at towre hylle, Cromwelle for tresone and lorde Hungerforthe for bockery.

And the xxx. day of the same monyth was doctor Barnes, Jerome and Garrard draune frome the tower in to Smythfelde, and there burnyd for their heryses. And that same day also was draune from the tower with them doctor Powell with two other prestes,[a] and there was a gallowys set up at sent Bartylmewys gate, and there ware hongyd, heddyd, and qwarterd that same day, and their qwarters sett abowte the cytte.

And the iiij. day of August was drawne from the tower to Tyborne, Gyllys Horne gentleman, Clement Phylpot, Edmonde Bromhame, Derby Kenhame, William Horne, Robert Byrde, Jarvys Garrow, and there hongyd, heddyd, and qwarterd, and their qwarteres with their heddes sett up abowte the citte.

xxxij°. A°. Thys yere was draune from the tower to Tyborne the xxij. day of December [Ralph] Egertone and Thomas Harman for cleppynge of golde,[b] and there hongyd, heddyd, and qwarterd, and their qwarteres set up.

Also the xxviij. day of June [1541] was be-heddyd at Towre hyll lorde Lenarde Graye markes,[c] and burryd within the tower.

And the xxix. of the same monyth was lorde Dakers[d] of the Sowth ledde with the shreffes of London unto Tyborne at after-none, and there hongyd for the new acte that was made, and browte home agayne in the carte unto sent Pulkeres and ther burryd.

And the xxviij. day of June was hongyd at sent Thomas Watterrynge, Mantell, Frudus and another.

[a] Abell, Powell, and Featherstone. Their religious tenets were directly opposed to those of the victims of the preceding day; but they were equally offensive to king Henry in denying his supremacy.

[b] Their crime was counterfeiting the king's seal in lead : see Stowe.

[c] *i. e.* son of the marquess of Dorset. He suffered, says Fabyan, "for divers treasons done in Ireland while he was the king's deputy there."

[d] Lord Dacre was hung for a murder committed in Sussex, as were his three companions named in the next paragraph.

Item the xxviij. day of May was the counteys of Salsbery be-hedyd within the tower.

xxxiij°. A°. Thys yere the x. daye of December was draune from the tower to Tyborne [Thomas] Colpeper, and there was hongyd and heddyd.

And the xiij. day of February [1542] was the qwene Kateryne and lady Rocheford be-heddyd within the tower, and there burryd.

And the xxviij. day of March there was a fraye made at the cown-ter in Bredstret of a sergant at harmes of the parlament howse by Robert Tomsone the yeman and Thomas Craker of the same howse for arest of Robert Taylor sergant of maysse, the wyche master shreffes ware sent for to the cowncelle, and they ware send unto the tower of London, and were there a iij. or iiij. dayes.

And the x. day of March was a mayde boyllyd in Smythfelde for poysynyng of dyvers persons.

And this yere came in the erle of Desmonde and the gret aNele, and was creatyd erle of Terone and hys sonne barone of Doncannen.

xxxiiij°. A°. Thys yere in October [1543] was a grete skermyche in the North abowte Carlelle, and many of the Scottys lordes tane and browte to London unto the tower the xx[ti]. day, and the nexte day ware browte unto the kynge and sworne to be trewe, and soo was ransomed and send home agayne.

And this yere was a grete pestelens in London, and Myhylmas terme remevyd un to sent Albons, and it beganne not tyll sent Mar-tyns day the xv. day of November.

Also the iij[de]. day of August before was proclamyd opyn warre betweene our kynge and the Frenche kynge.

And this yere was a gret derth for wode and colles.

xxxv°. A°. Thys yere the xxiij. day of December at none rysse a gret tempest of wynde and rayne, and contynewyd all the nyght tyll the nexte daye at viij. of the clocke, and in that tyme was moch harme on the see that lost manny sheppes of merchantes and grete men and women of Spanyarddes that ware goynge un to the empe-ror agay[nst] Chrystmas, and the[y] with all their goodes ware drownyd and lost and gast up, as dyvers persons both men and women; and that tyme came the kynge of Costelle in to Ynglond,[a] and came by watter un to the Whytt halle un to the kynge, and soo un to Rychemond, and was there tylle the furst day of Januarij [1544], and thene departyd home agayne and had grete geftes gevyne hym.

And on tewelfe day in the mornyng beganne a grette myst that a man myght not see a two yerddes before hym, and then was moche harme done in the see that dyvers sheppes ware lost and tane by Frenche men, and some in to this lond.

And at this tyme was worde browte un to the kynge that the erle of Angwyche[b] in Scotlonde, whome the kynge had kepte hym with his brother and dyvers other here in Ynglond more thane a vj. or vij. yeres, and had hym with the other lordes of Scotlonde sworne[c] and resevyd the sacrament that thei shulde be trew, and soo went home, and the erle of Angwyche was made captayne of Barwyke; and at thys tyme he stale awaye and carryd with hym the principalle of the ordenans, with plate, monny, harnes, horse, and wettelles, and went in to Scotland to a castelle of hys with the other lordes wyth hym un to the byshoppe of sent Andrewys, agayne[d] our master the kynge of Ynglond, whome had cherycyd and made moche of theme alle and gave theme many grete yeffttes, and they lyke traytors dyssevyd hym and the reme wyth their false crafftes.

Also the vij. day of Marche was draune from the tower of London un to Tyborne v. prestes and [Germaine] Gardner cecretore un to the byshoppe of Wynchester, and theis ware the prestes names *(left blank)*; and there ware hongyd, heddyd, and qwarterd, and their qwarteres with their heddes byrryd there.

And the xix. day of March was draune from the tower unto Tyborne . . . . . Ascheby, that was some tyme a prest and forsoke it, and there was hongyd and qwarterd and there byrryd.

[a] See a note on this event in the Chronicle of Calais, p. 5.

[b] Archibald Douglas, the husband of the dowager Queen Margaret.

[c] shorne *in MS.*

[d] *i. e.* against.

Also the last day of Aprille dyde the lord Thomas Audle chauncheler of Yngloṅd, and for hym was made lorde Thomas Wresley.

Item, the xvj. day of May was made a proclamacion in London for raysynge of golde and sylver, as the ryalle xij. shillings, and the angelle at viij. shillings, and sylver at iiij. shillings the unce; and also that alle French men shuld voyde the realme within xx. dayes or elles to be made free denycens, under payene of deth; and a new qwyne of sylver, of xij[d]. apece, grottes, and ij[d]. with hole facis.[a]

Item, the xxij. day of May was the Assencion day, and at nyght was made grete bone-fyers thorrow all London, and grete chere in every parych at every bone-fyer, and grete melody with dyvers instrewmentes; and the mayer with the shreffes rydynge thorrow every warde of London to see how it was done, for the good tydynges that came owte of Scotlond.

Item, this yere was no wache at Mydsomer be cause of the warres; but the mayer wyth the shereffes rode thorrow alle London, and every alderman in hys warde with the constabulles.

And this yere the kynges grace went un to Bollen, and layd sege there to the xix. day of July, and lay there tyll it was the xiij. day of September, and as that day it was yeldyd up un to the kynges grace, and the kynge gave them alle there lyffes and pardynd them to goo with bagge and bagges, and lent them apon a vij. score waggens or more to carré ther stoffe, and soo went awaye in to France. But the vij. day of October they came agayne unto basse Bullene and there slew all the Englyche men, women and chelderne, and sett it alle a fyer, and went their wayes agayne. And there was tane the captayne of grete Bullyne and dyvers of ours with them.[b]

xxxvj°. A°. Thys yere the ix[th] day of December was vij. gentylmen of Kent sett on the pyllerẏ at the stondard in Cheppe, and stode there three owers, and there here cut by the erys, and one of eche of

[a] *i. e.* with front faces, as distinguished from "half-faces," in which the king's head was figured in profile.

[b] These four last lines are erased in the MS.

ther erys cut of, and burnyd in the cheke, and then tane downe and had un to pressone; and after that carryd un to Maydson,[a] and there in the markyd place set on the pyllory and the other eyrs cut of, and burnyd in the other cheke, and then had un to preson; and there remaynyd un to soch tyme as they had made bonddes un to the kynge of payment of soche mony as was taxit un to them by the kynge and hys cowncell.

And the xv. day of the same monthe at nyght was caste dyvers bokys of eryses in dyvers [parts of] London agayne the sacrament of the auter with all other sacramenttes and sacramentalles, and namynge dyvers tymes the byshoppe of Wynchester,[b] with dyvers other byshoppes and lernede men, with gret rebukes dyvers tymes in it of them.

Also this yere the xij. of Januarij beganne the gatherynge of the benyvolens at Baynysse castelle[c] for the kynges warrys.

And also before Crystmas was moche wyne tane of France with ther shyppes and layed in the church sumtyme the Gray freeres, all the church fulle in every place of it, and at the Austyn freeres and the Blacke freeres wyth herrynge and other fyche that was tane on the see goynge in to France that came from Anwarppe.

And this yere was an alderman of London made a captayne in to Scotlond, Rede a scalter.[d] And this same yere the Scottes toke a grete multitudyne of the Ynglych pepulle and slew them alle shamfully.

And thys yere stode a prest of Kente at Polles crose for cuttynge of hys fynger and made it to blede on the hoste at his masse for a fallse sacrafyce; and also another prest this yere was sett on the

[a] Maidstone.

[b] Stephen Gardiner.

[c] Baynard's Castle, in the city of London.

[d] Holinshed relates of the battle at Pannyer haugh in March 1544-5, that among other prisoners taken by the Scotishmen "Richard Read an alderman of London was one, who, for that he refused to pay such a sum of money as the commissioners for the benevolence demanded of him, was commanded forthwith to serve the king in his wars against the Scots, and so was taken now at this overthrow." This unfortunate alderman seems never to have arrived at the dignity of lord mayor, or even sheriff.

pyllere in Chepe for makynge of false letters in the weste contre un to a blynde woman.

And this yere was no wache at Mydsomer for be cause of the warres bothe in France and also in Scotlonde.

And this yere was the church of the Whytfreeres pullyd downe, and the stepulle of the Blacke freeres, and yt was stoppyd up [with lede agayne, and the waye[a]] goynge un to Baynysche castell from the sayd freeres.

And this yere was the Mary Rose lost beside Porchmew, with dyvers captayns, as sir George Carrow with many dyvers other.[b]

Also the 22. day of June was a grete moster of the cytte of London, and that same day in the mornynge was dyvers howsys a fyer at Algate.

Also the xix. day of the same monythe before beganne at ix. of the cloke at nyght a gret rayene with thonder and lyghtnynge, and contenewyd un to the next day at x. of the cloke.

Item the xij. day of September at iiij. of cloke in the mornynge was sent Gylles church at Creppyll gatte burnyd, alle hole save the walles, stepull, belles and alle, and how it came God knoweth.[c]

Item thys same yere in the same monyth was the Charterhowse pulde downe, and the watter turned to dyvers places ther to gentylmens placys.[d]

Item the 23. daye of the same monyth was a gret generalle processione of alle parsons, vekeres, curattes, with alle other prestes in every church, clarkes alle in copys and a crosse of every churche,

[a] A second hand has inserted these words.

[b] Of this accident the fullest account is that in the memoirs of sir Peter Carew in the Archæologia, vol. xxviii. p. 111. Several guns were recovered from the wreck so recently as the year 1839, (vide ibid. p. 386,) and are now preserved at Woolwich.

[c] This church escaped the great fire of 1666, and now contains many interesting memorials of the previous century.

[d] This refers to the conduit at the Charter-house, the water of which was derived from the White Conduit fields. A very curious ancient plan of the pipes is still preserved at the Charter-house, a fac-simile of which by Vertue is in the portfolio of the Society of Antiquaries, and a reduced engraving has been published in The Carthusian, 1839, p. 498.

and soo went up un to Ledyne halle one the onsyde, with alle Powles in their copys and the byshoppe in his myttor, with alle the crafftes in theire best lyverys, and soo downe one the other syde, and soo to Powlles agayne. And that same day stode one on the pyllery at the stonderd in Cheppe for mysse-usyng of the kynges comyssion. And the occasion of the procession was (*unfinished*).

xxxvij°. A°. Thys yere the xxvj. day of Februarij was browth from the towre of London thorrow the cytte in to Smythfelde, with the shreffes and offesars, and there browth unto the stake wher as was fyer, for clyppynge of golde, and there had hare pardone, and soo was hadde unto the tower agayne thorrow sent Bartelmewys spyttylle.[a]

Item the xiij. day of June after was Wytsonsonday, and then was a generalle processione from Powlles un to sent Peters in Cornehylle with alle the chelderne of Powlles scole, and a crosse of every parishe churche, with a banner and one to ber it in a tenache, alle the clarkes, alle the presttes, with parsons and vekeres of every church in coppys, and the qwere of Powlles in the same maner, and the byshoppe bereynge the sacrament under a canapy with the mayr in a gowne of cremsone velvet, the aldermen in scarlet, with alle the crafttes in their best aparelle; and whan the mayer came betwene the crosse and the standert there was made a proclamacyon with dyvers harhoddes of armes and pursevanttes in their cote armeres, with the trompettes, and ther was proclamyd a unyversalle pes for ever betwene the emperar, the kynge of Ynglonde, the French kynge, and alle crystyne kynges for ever.

Item the xj. day of Aprille before was Passion sonday, and then preched doctor Crome[b] in hys pariche church, at the wyche sermond he preched agayne the sacrament of the auter; and that same tyme he was send for unto the corte, and there was exammynd; and the v. sarmondes at Ester spake alle agayne the sayd oppynyons, but namyd not hym. And the sonday after the Low sonday, the wyche

[a] The chronicler does not give the woman's name.

[b] Edward Crome, S.T.P. rector of Saint Mary Aldermary.

was the ix. day of May after, he preched at Powlles crosse, and there sayd he came not thether to recante nor to denye hys worddes nor wolde not. And then he was send for that same day agayne, and was examynd agayne; and the xxvij[ti]. day of June after, wyche was the sonday after Corpus Christi day, he was comandyd to preche at Powlles crosse agayne, and there recantyd and denyyd hys worddes, as yow shall have in hys artycles with other moo at the end of the boke.[a]

And the xvj. day of July was burnyd in Smythfelde for grett herrysy . . . . Hemmysley a prest, wyche was an Observand freere of Richemond; Anne Askew, otherwyse callyd Anne Kyme by hare husband;[b] John Lassellys, a gentylman of Furnevalles inne; and a taylor of Colchester. And Nicolas Schaxton some tyme byshopp of Salsbery was one of the same company, and was in Newgat and had juggement with them; Blacke, gentylman; and Christopher Whytt, of the inner tempull; these iij. had their pardon. And Schaxtone preched at their burnynge, and there satt on a scaffold that was made for the nonse the lorde chaunsler[c] with the dewke of Norfoke and other of the cownsell, with the lorde mayer, dyvers aldermen and shreffes, and the jugges.

Item the furst day of August after preched at Powlles cross the sayd Nicolas Schaxton, and there recantyd, and wepte sore and made grete lamentacion for hys offens, and pray[ed] the pepulle alle there to for-geve hym hys mysse insample that he had gevyn un to the pepulle.

Item the xx[ti]. day of the same monyth after came in the lorde amrelle of France[d] un to Grenwych with xiiij. goodly gallys, and many other sheppes, and there was shotte many gonnys; and soo the nexte day came be watter un to the tower wharffe, and so came

[a] These articles are not contained in the MS. from which we are now printing. Dr. Crome survived this persecution, and died in 1562, still holding his rectory. Newcourt.

[b] Anne Askew, or Ascough, was the daughter of Sir William Ascough, of Kelsey in Lincolnshire, and had been married to Mr. Kyme of the same county, but had ceased to live with him; whence the ambiguity of the designation.

[c] Sir Thomas Wriothesley.

[d] Claude de Honnebald: compare with an account of this embassy in Holinshed.

thorrow the cytte; and in Cheppe-syde betwene the crosse and sent Myhylles stode the mayer with alle the aldermen and the crafftes in their best lyverys, and the mayer gave hym a present in the name of alle the cytte; and soo came un to the byshoppes pallys of London, and lay there sonday alle day; and the monday was Bartylmew-evyn, and then he was had to Hamton corte where the kynges grace lay, and there was ryally resevyd and had grete chere with many grete jefftes;[a] and soo laye there tyll ytt was the fryday after; and then departyd, and came agayn unto London; and the monday after in the mornynge departyd, and soo went home agayne with grete joye.

Item the xxvj. day of September was burnyd at Powlles crosse a gret multytude of Ynglych bokes, as testamenttes and other bokes, the wych ware forbodyn by proclamacyon by the kynges commandment before, thorrow alle hys domynyon.

Also at thys tyme was made an acte in the cytte that ever more after that they shulde chose the mayer of the sayd cytte on Myhylmas day; and here it beganne furst; and then was made an acte that there shulde be no more mayer's fest but thoys that wolde kepe it.

xxxviij°. A°. Thys yere the xijth day of December the dewke of Norffoke and the yerle of Sorré hys sonne ware comyttyd unto the tower of London, and the dewke went be watter from the lorde chaunselers place in Holborne that was sometyme the byshoppe of Ely's, and soo downe un to the watter syde, and so be watter un to the tower; and hys sonne the yerle of Sorré went thorrow the cytte of London, makynge grete lamentacion.[b]

Item the xx^{ti} day of the same monyth was draune from Newgate un to the tower hyll for qwynynge of the kynges mony, there was hongyd and no more.[c]

[a] gifts.

[b] This probably means that the sight of the earl in disgrace caused great commiseration and lamentation.

[c] Again, the person or persons are not described by the chronicler.

Item the 13. day of Januarij was the yerle of Sorrey browte from the tower of London un to the yelde-halle of London, and there he was from ix. unto yt was v. at nyght, and there had hys juggement to be heddyd; and soo the xix. day of the some month it was done at the Towre hylle.

Item the 3°. day of Januarij was sette opyn the churche agayen that was sometyme the Grayfreeres, and masse sayd at the auteres wyth dyvers presttes, and it was namyd Crystys churche of the fundacion of kynge Henry the viijth.

EDWARDUS SEXTUS REX.

Item the 31. day of the same monyth was proclamyd kynge Edward the Sixth, and came the same day unto the tower of London. And kynge Henry the eighth dyde at the manor of Whytte halle at Westmyster. And the xiiij. day of February was browte from thens on to Syone and there laye alle nyght, and the nexte day browth un to Wynsore and there byrryd by qwene Jane.

Item the xx. day of the same monyth the sayd kynge Edwarde the sixth came from the tower of London thorrow London, and in dyvers places pagenttes, and alle the strettes hangyd reghely,[a] wyth alle the crafftes stondynge in Chepe, presentynge them as lovynge subjecttes unto their kynge, and soo to Powlles; and at the west ende of Powlles stepull was tayed a cabelle roppe, and the other ende besyde the denes place at an hanker of a sheppe,[b] and a man ronnynge downe on the sayd roppe as swefte as an arrow owte of a bowe downe wyth hys honddes and fette abrode not tochynge the roppe; and whane the kynge had sene the sayd thynge went forth un to the pallys of Westmyster; and the nexte day came from thens unto Westmyster churche, and there was crownyd, and kepte hys fest in Westmyster halle. God of hys mercy sende hym good locke and longe lyffe, with prosperite! And this was done in the ix. yere of hys age and byrth. And at that ryallty was made sir Edward

[a] richly. [b] A ship's anchor.

Semer that was yerle of Harforth duke of Somerset, and protector and defender of the realme; and sir Thomas Semer hys brother lorde governer un to the kyng;[a] and sir Thomas Worthesle that was at that tyme lorde chaunseler of Ynglond was made yerle of Sowthhamtone; and sir John Dudley that was amrelle of the see was made yerle of Warwyk.[b] And iiij. or v. dayes after was gret justes at Westmyster.

Item the xix. day of June after was a sollome dyrege at Powles for the French kynge,[c] with a goodly herse in the qwere, and the lorde of Arnedel principalle morner, with dyvers byshoppes, the mayer of London with the aldermen, and alle the hed crafftes of London, and alle the qweer, with the boddy of the church hangyd with blacke clothe and hys armys, and ij C. powre men in blacke gownes holdynge staffe torches; and the nexte day the sayd obbyt kepte in every paryche churche in London wyth the belles ryngyng.

Item the v. day after in September beganne the kynges vysytacion at Powlles, and alle imagys pullyd downe; and the ix. day of the same monyth the sayd visytacion was at sent Bryddes, and after that in dyvers other paryche churches; and so alle imagys pullyd downe thorrow alle Ynglonde att that tyme, and alle churches new whytte-lymed, with the commandmenttes wryttyne on the walles. And at that tyme was the byshoppe of London[d] put into the Flette, and was there more than viij. dayes; and after hym was the byshoppe of Wenchester[e] put there also.

Item at this same tyme was pullyd up alle the tomes, grett stones, alle the auteres, with the stalles and walles of the qweer and auteres in the church that was some tyme the Gray freeres, and solde, and the qweer made smaller.[f]

Thys yere the iiij[th] day of November bagan the parlement at Westmyster, and before this parlament the lord Richard Ryche was

[a] *These words are erased and* amrelle *written in the margin.*

[b] *An early hand has altered this to* made erlle of Warwyke and governor to the kynge.

[c] Francis I.

[d] Edmund Bonner.

[e] Stephen Gardiner.

[f] See the Prefatory Note on the Grey Friars.

made chaunseler of Ynglond, and the lord Sent Jone that was lorde grandmaster gave it up.

Item the xvij. day of the same monythe at nyghte was pullyd downe the Rode in Powlles with Mary and John, with all the images in the churche, and too of the men that labord at yt was slayne and dyvers other sore hurtte. Item also at that same time was pullyd downe throrrow alle the kynges domynyon in every churche alle Roddes with alle images, and every precher preched in their sermons agayne alle images. Also the newyeresday after preched *doctor* [a] Latemer that some tyme was byshop of Wysseter preched at Powlles crosse, and too sondayes followyn, &c. Also this same tyme was moche spekyng agayne the sacrament of the auter, that some callyd it Jacke of the boxe, with divers other shamfulle names; and then was made a proclamacyon agayne shoche sayers, and it (*sc.* yet) bothe the prechers and other spake agayne it, and so contynewyd; and at Ester followyng there began the commonion, and confession but of thoys that wolde, as the boke dothe specifythe. And at this tyme was moche prechyng agayne the masse. And the sacrament of the auter pullyd downe in dyvers placys thorrow the realme. Item after Ester beganne the servis in Ynglyche [at Powles at the commandment of the dene at the tyme, William May, [b]] and also in dyvers other pariche churches. Item also at Wytsontyde beganne the sermons at sent Mary spyttylle. Item also this yere was Barkyng chappylle at the Towre hylle pullyd downe, and sent Martyns at the chambulles end, sent Nicolas in the chambulles, and sent Ewyns, and within the gatte of Newgate thoys [c] were put un to the churche that some tyme was the Gray Freres; and also Strand churche [d] also pullyd downe to make the protector duke of Somerset's place larger.

[a] This word is erased.

[b] These words are added in a sidenote.

[c] *i. e.* the inhabitants of St. Sepulchre's parish residing eastward of Newgate, as well as the parishioners of the two churches last named, were transferred to the new parish of Christ church.

[d] This was called the church of Saint Mary and the Holy Innocents. It was a parish church, and the parishioners were at first joined to those of St. Clement's Danes, and afterwards to the church of St. John the Baptist in the Savoy, until their own church was re-erected in the reign of queen Anne.

Item this yere was alle the chaunterys put downe.

Item also the wacche at mydsomer was begonne agayne, that was left from M. Dodmer[a] un to this tyme.

Item also the byshoppe of Wenchester at that tyme Stephyn Gardner preched before the kyng at sent James in the felde on sent Petter's day at afternone the wyche was then fryday, and on the morrow after was commytted unto the tower of London to warde.

Item the vij. day of July after there was a prest that came owte of Cornewalle drawne from the towre of London unto Smythefelde, and there was honged and heddyd and qwarterd for sleying of one Boddy[b] that was the kynges commyssyoner in that contry for chauntries.

Item, alle thoys prechers that prechyd at Powlles crosse at that tyme spake moche agayne the bysshoppe of Wynchester; and also Cardmaker,[c] that rede in Powlles iij. tymes a weke, had more or lesse of hym.

Item this same yere was put downe alle goyng abrode of processyons, and the sensyng at Powlles at Wytsontyde, and the Skynners' processyon on Corpus Christi day, with alle others, and had none other but the Ynglyche procession in their churches.

Item at this tyme was moche prechyng thorro alle Ynglonde agayne the sacrament of the auter, save only M. Laygton, and he preched in every place that he prechyd agayne them alle; and so was moche contraversy and moche besynes in Powlles every sonday, and syttyng in the churche, and of none that were honest persons, but boyes and persons of lyttylle reputacyon; and wolde have made m[oche] mor yf there had not a way a bene tane. And at the last the xxviij. [day] of December[d] followyng there was a proclamacyon that none of bothe partyes shulde preche un to soche tyme as the counselle had determyned soche thynges as they were in hond with alle: for as that tyme dyvers of the bysshoppes sat at Cherse abbe for dyvers matters of the kynge and the counselle.

[a] Ralph Dodmer was sheriff in 1524, the 16th Hen. VIII.

[b] William Body: see Strype, Memorials, ii. 91.

[c] John Cardmaker, vicar of St. Bride's, afterwards burnt in 1555.

[d] December *is erased, but the marginal correction is burnt away from the MS.*

Item the iij[de]. [day of] the same monyth was browte from Hygate unto London unto the laumpe in Ne[wgate] market a monstre, a calfe wyth ij. heddes, iiij. eres, iiij. eyne, viij. f[eete] and ij. taylles; that there the mayer wyth dyvers aldermen came thether and saue it, and command[ed] yt to be browte into the stret and there he saue it, and there command[ed] it to be carred into the feldes strayt wayes and to be cutte in peces, and put into the grownde, and soo it was.

Also at that tyme was many ballyttes made of dyvers partys agayne the blyssyd sacrament, one agayne another, and the too pers[ons] that redde in Powlles, as Cardmaker and one that rede tewsday and thursday in Latten, spake agayne the sacrament, and sayd it was but brede and wynne.

Item this yere before Alhallontyd was sett up the howse for the markyt folke in Newgate market for to waye melle in.

Item also this yere was put downe the chappell with the charnell howse in Powlles church yerde, with the too tomes one the north syde, and a iiij. or v. C. lode of bones carred in to the feldes and burryd there.

ij°. A°. Thys yere on sent Martyns day begane the sarmond at the crosse agayne, and there was the byshoppe of sent Davys one Farrar,[a] but he dyd not preche in hys abbet of a byshoppe, but lyke a prest, and he spake agayne all maner of thynges of the churche and the sacrament of the auter, and vestmenttes, coppes, alterres, with alle other thynges, &c.

Item the xxij. day of November was in the nyghte a grete fyer in the tower of London, and a gret pesse burnyd, by the menes of a Frencheman that sette a barrelle of gonnepoder a fyere, and soo was burnyd hymselfe, and no more persons, but moch hurte besyde; and the xxiiij[ti]. day of the same monyth was sent Annes church at Aldersgate burnyd.

Item at Newyeeres tyde after was put downe the qwyne of the testornes.

[a] Robert Ferrar.

Item the x. day of December was drawne from Newgate unto Towre hylle *(blank)* and there ware hongyd for qwyneynge of testornes.

Item the xvij. day of January was commytted un to the tower lorde Thomas Semer that was lorde amrelle, with dyvers other, for hye tresone, as yt shalbe declaryd afterwarde.

Item the viij. day of March a bucher of sent Nicolas shambulles was put on the pyllery in Cheppesyde for kepynge of another buchers wyffe in the same strette, and there stode iiij. oweres and more.

Item the xx. day of Marche was sir Thomas [Seym]er that was lorde amrelle was be-hedyd at the Towre hylle for hye [treason].

The ij^de sonday of Lent preched Coverdalle, and whan hye masse was done the dene of Powlles that was that tyme William May commandyd the sacrament at the hye autre to be pullyd downe.

Item the vj. day of Aprille was a proclamacion for the masse, [and for] ettynge of fleshe agayne May day, but for the fleshe was nothynge kepte.

Item the vij. day after was a grete and marvelus wynde both in the nyght and also in [the] day.

Item the x. day of Aprill was pullyd downe the clowster in Powlles that was callyd the Pardon churcheyerd wyth the chappelle that stode in the myddes, to bylde the protectores place with alle.

Item the xxij. of Aprille was the monday in Ester weke, and that nyght was burnyd fyve howsys at Brokenwharfe.

Item the xxvij. day of Aprill, the whych was the satorday in Ester weke, the ante-baptystes ware in our Lady chappelle in Powlles before *the byshoppe of Caunterbory with other comyssioners,*[a] and there one recantyd; and the nexte sonday, the wych was Lowe sonday, stode at the crosse and bare a faggott. Item the nexte sattorday after the byshoppe wyth the resydew of the commyssyoners satt agayne. And there was one Jone of Kente other wyse Jone Bucher

[a] These words are erased in the MS.

condemnyd; and a tanner of Colchester recantyd, and nexte day bare a faggotte at the crosse, and the nexte sonday at Colchester. And that day stode at the crosse a boccher of Mary Maudlyne parich in Fychstret,[a] and the nexte sonday agayne for be cause he made a mocke at the furst tyme.

Item the iij. day of June, the wyche was the monday after the Assencion day, alle the gray ammesse[b] with the calober in Powlles ware put downe.

Item the xx[ti] day of June, the wyche was Corpus Christi day, and as that day in dyvers places in London was kepte holy day, and manny kepte none, but dyd worke opynly, and in some churches servys and some none, soche was the devysyon.

Item in this yere moche pepulle of the comyns dyd ryse in dyvers places in the realme, and pullyd downe parkes and growndes that was inclosyd of dyvers lordes and gentylmen within the realme from the powre men.

Item the xxvij. day of June there was sent a commandement from the councelle unto Powlles that they shulde have no more the Apostylles masse in the mornynge, nor our Lady masse, nor no communyone at no aultelle in the church but at the hye awlter.

Item the xviij. day of July, wher as there was a boke made and send up to the commyns of Cornwalle and Devynshere with alle other parttes of all the realme for be cause of their rysynge and pullynge downe of incloseres, the wyche was some tyme comyns un to the powre men, and grette men toke theme in and inclosyd it to them and made parkes in dyvers places, and as thys tyme the commyns for the most parte within the realme ryssyd and pullyd up heggys and palys and sett yt opyn a gayne; and then the boke was send unto them that they shuld be content gentylly, and within shortte space it shulde be mendyd, and so to submytte them selfes

[a] Old Fish Street.

[b] The canons, so called from their tippets (see the glossarial note at the close of Machyn's Diary, p. 461.) The calober was apparently another portion of their furred vestment; see the passage quoted in the same place relative to the aldermen.

and to aske mercy and pardone; and this day abovesayd it was proclamyd thorrow alle London both with harhalde and trompeters, and so was send unto alle the partys of the realme wher as they dyde ryse, and in-mediatly after the sayd proclamacion if they dyd submytte them selfes and aske mercy and pardon they shuld have it, and if not they shulde be tane as traytores and to be subdewyd with the [sword]. And as that same tyme all the gattes of the citte of London was layed with grett gonnes with-in the citte warte,[a] and within the sayed gattes both above and beneth in dyvers parttes, with dyvers artyllery ryght good, and their percullys new made at dyvers gattes, and both[b] at Newgate n[ew] made strongly. And every daye from the xx. day of July satte at every gatte viij. of the comyneres and ij. gonners every day from vj. in the mornynge unto it was . . . . . atte nyght unto the x. day of September.

Item the xxj. day of the same monyth, the wyche was sonday, the byshoppe of Cauntorbery[c] came sodenly to Powlles, and there shoyd and made a narracyon of thoys that dyd rysse in dyvers places within the realme, and what rebellyous they were, and wolde take aponne them to reforme thynges befor the lawe, and to take the kynges powre in honde. And soo was there at procession, and dyd the offes hym selfe in a cope and no vestment, nor mytter, nor crosse, but a crose staffe; and soo dyd alle the offes, and hys sattene cappe on hys hede alle the tyme of the offes; and soo gave the communione hym selfe unto viij. persons of the sayd church.

Also the xxij. day of the same monyth, the wyche was Mary Maudlyne day, there was hongyd one that came from Romford, on a gybbytt at the welle within Algate; and another that came owte of Kent at the brygge fotte in to Sothwarke on another gybbytte, that ware of the same persons and company.

Item the xxiij. day of the same monyth the kynges grace came from the dewke of Soffokes place in Sothwarke thorrow London, and soo to Whytte hall goodly, with a goodly company.

[a] ward. [b] gates? [c] Thomas Cranmer.

Item the xxviij. day and the xxix. day was dyvers persons conventyd before the counselle because of hereynge of masse at Crycherch[a] wheras the French imbassetors laye, that they shuld come no more there, and was gretly rebukyd.

Item the iiij. day of August, the wyche was sonday, was men sett a worke from Newgate alle alonge by the citte walles to pulle downe the gardyns that was made a longe by the walles of the citte with howses, and soo alle alonge unto *(blank)*.

Item the furst day of August was a gret battelle at Norwych betwene the lorde markes of Northamtone and the comyns that dyd aryse there, and manny was slayene of both partys, and the lorde markes put un to flyette, and the lorde Cheffelde[b] slayne, with many dyvers knyttes and many other good men. And many of the sayed comyns slayne and tane prisoneres.

Item the *(blank)* day of the same monyth was a battell be syde Exceter be-twene the lorde Rosselle that was then lorde privisele, lorde Graye, and the comyns of that cuntre; and many slayne and tane prisoneres of both partyes.

Item the ix. day of the same monyth was proclamyd in the curte by ane imbassitor of France wyth a harhalde and trompetter opyn warre, and that same nyght was tane alle Frenche men that ware noe free denysens, and an inventory of alle their goodes, and put in prison thorrow alle the realme at that tyme.

Item the x. day of the same monyth the byshoppe of Cauntorbery came and preched at Powlles, the wych was sattorday, in the qwere in the byshoppes stalle that he was wonte to be stallyd in, for them that [rose] in the West contre of the comyns of Devynchere and Cornewalle, and there he shoyd that the occasyone cam of poppych prestes was the most parte of alle hys sermond.

[a] The house of Augustinian canons of the Holy Trinity within Aldgate was commonly called Christchurch or Creechurch, and a neighbouring church in Leadenhall Street is still named St. Katharine Creechurch. After the dissolution this house was granted in 1533 to lord chancellor Audley, and in the reign of queen Elizabeth we find it occupied by the duke of Norfolk, in Machyn's Diary, pp. 186, 294.

[b] Edmund first lord Sheffield.

Item the xv. day of the same monyth, the Assumcyon of our Lady, and that day was hongyd too persons, one withowte Algate and the other at Totnam hylle; and as that day some kepte holydaye and some none, as sent Stevyns in Walbroke and Colcherch, soch was the devysion that day, as it was on Corpus Christi day.

Item the xviij. day of the same monyth the bysshoppe of London[a] dyd the offes at Powlles both at the processyon and the comunione dyscretly and sadly.

Item on Bartylmew evyne was shott dyvers goonnes at the gattes in London.

Item this yere was no cheesys in Bartylmew fayer but soch as came owte of dyvers mens howsys within London that was not good, and the cause was for them that rose in Essex as that tyme.

Item the xxvij. day of the same monyth was iij. persons drawyn, hongyd, and qwarterd at Tyborne, that came owte of the West contre.

Item the xxviij. day of the same monythe was a woman delyveryd of ij. chelderne at Bodyly a smyth at the Longlane ende in Smythfelde, and whan the woman was delyveryd she desyred to se hare chelderne, and the wyffe of the howse sayd they ware saffe inowgh, and she toke one of them and brake the necke of yt, and caused the mayd of the howse to take the other and to cast it over the walle, and so dystroyd them bothe; and then was the woman that had the chelderne, and the wyffe of the howse and the mayde, ware had to the cownter in Bredstrete, and there the woman was delyveryd of another chylde that same nyghte.

Item the last day of the same monyth the byshoppe of Cauntorbery[b] shulde a come agayne to Powlles, and a preched agayne, but he send Josephe[c] hys chaplyne, and he preched in the qwere of the subdewynge of them that dyd rysse in alle iij. places, and how mysery they ware browte unto, and there he rehersyd as hys master dyd before that the occasyone came by popysse presttes.

[a] Edmund Bonner.

[b] Thomas Cranmer.

[c] John Joseph, S.T.P. collated to the rectory of St. Mary le Bow by archbishop Cranmer, Oct. 20, 1546.

Item the furst day of September the byshoppe of London then Edmund Boner preched at Powlles crosse, and after was acuysyd un to the cownsell by too persons, as William Latymer [a] parsone of sent Lawrens Powntney and John Hopper [b] that some tyme was a whyth monnke, and soo was conventyd before the byshope of Cauntorbery wyth other comyssoneres the xiij. day of the same monyth, and the xvj. day and the xviij.; and the xx[ti] day of the same moneth at nyght he was send unto the Marchese,[c] and he went the same day unto Lambythe in hys scarlet habbet and hys rochett aponne it.

Item this same day Cardmaker sayd opynly in hys lector in Powlles that if God ware a man he was a vj. or vij. foote of lengthe, with the bredth, and if it be soo how canne it be that he shuld be in a pesse of brede in a rownde cake on the awter: what an ironyos oppynyone is this unto the leye pepulle!

At this tyme doctor Smyth [d] rebukyd the byshehoppe gretly, and the byshoppe dyd nothynge gretly forbore hym, and gave hym many chockynge worddes opynly.[e]

Item the xxij. of the same monyth the byshoppe of Cauntorbery causyd Hopper to preche at Powlles crosse, and there he spake moch agayne the byshope of London. And the xxiij. day was there [f] before the sayd commysyoners agayne.

And the xxv. day Cardmaker rede in Powlles, and sayd in hys lector that he cowde not rede there the xxvij. day for because he must neddes be at the sessyons as that day at Lambythe for the byshoppe of London; but it was not soo, for the byshoppe came not there. Item the xxix. of the same monyth preched in the shrowddes, for because of rayne, one Golde, and he spake moche agaynst the sayd byshoppe of London, and there stode be-fore hym one that dwellyd in Charterus lane wyth a screpture on hys brest for coungerynge.

[a] Afterwards dean of Peterborough.

[b] Afterwards bishop of Worcester and Gloucester.

[c] Marshalsea.

[d] Richard Smith, regius professor of divinity at Oxford.

[e] This is printed as in the MS. The writer apparently wishes to represent the great violence of doctor Smith, and the great forbearance of bishop Bonner.

[f] *i. e.* apparently the bishop.

Item the furst day of October the byshoppe of London was send for at after-none unto Lambythe, and ther the byshoppe of Cauntorbery dyschargyd[a] the sayd byshopp of London as moche as laye in hys powre; but marke what followeth.

Item the vij. day of October was proclaymyd the protector a traytor, with all hys helperes, and that day begane agayne the watch[b] at every gatt in London of the comeneres in harnes with weppyns.

Item the viij. day it was proclamyd opynly with the kynges shreffe and two harraldes and two pursevanttes and a trumpet, with the comyne sargant of the citte of London, thorrow alle London, and as fast as it myght be thorrow alle Ynglond.

Item the nexte day Cardmaker sayd in hys lector, thow he[c] had a falle he was not undone, and that men shuld not have ther purpos; and also he sayd that men wolde have up agayne ther popych masse; wher for, good masteres, stycke unto yt hade[d] he sayd.

Item the xiij. day of the same monyth was no sermond at the crosse.

Item the xiiij. day at after-none was browth the traytor[e] from Wyndsor with a gret company of lorddes and gentylmen, and many horsys, with their men with weppyns, and came in at sent Gylles in the felde at hys desyre, for be cause he wolde not come by the place that he had begonne and pullyd downe dyvers churches and the clowster in Powlles to bylde yt with all, [and soo unto the tower of London with dyvers other prisoneres,[f]] but almyghty God wolde not suffer yt for hys gret myscheffe as it shalle evydently follow by hys actes. And whane he came in Chepesyde he sayd opynly, that manny pepull harde hym, that he was as trewe a man to the kynge as anny was there, evyn prowdly.

Item the xvij. day the kynges grace came from the place in

[a] *i. e.* deposed.

[b] washe *in MS.*

[c] *i. e.* the duke of Somerset.

[d] *So in MS.; q?* take unto it heed.

[e] The person so indignantly designated is the late Protector.

[f] These words are an insertion after the first writing.

Sothewarke thorrow London, and soo to Whytt halle; and that nyght was the comyneres of London was dyscharged of ther waching at alle the gattes of London in harnes, and to wache no more but the comyne wache as a nyttes in every warde as it hath bene acostomyd before.

iij°. A°. This yere the vj. day of December was Bodylys wyffe the smythes w[ife at Long lane] ende in Smythfelde hongyd at Tyborne for the dystrowynge of [her chil]derne at Bartylmewtyde as it shoyth before.

Item the vij. [day of Ja]nuary [1550] was vj. men dystroyd at the makynge of the welle wythin the howse that was some tyme the Peter college[a] nexte the denes place in Powlles churche yarde.

Item of the great gentylnes that was shoyd unto the byshope of London Edmund Boner beynge prisoner in the Marchelse the viij. day of January of the knyght marchalle takynge away hys bedde, and soo that he had no more to lye in but straw and a coverlet for the space of viij. days, for because he wolde not geve the knyght marchall x li. or a gowne of that price.

Item the xix. day of the same monythe at ix. a clocke at nyght was kyllyd captyne Gambolde a valyant man a Spanyerd and another with hym, and dyvers of their servanttes hurte, of another captyne[b] of hys owne contry-men; and was tane the nexte day and three more wyth hyme, and the xxij. day of the same monyth raynyd atte the yelde halle, and the xxiij. day they ware condemnyd, and the xxiiij. day they ware hongyd in the myddes of Smythfelde; and he that kyllyd captayne Gambolde, ther as the dede was done or ever he went in-to Smythfelde, ther hys hond was smyttyne of, and after was hongyd wyth the resydew in Smythfelde.

Item the xxvij. day of the same monyth was draune from the tower of London un-to Tyborne iiij. persons, and there hongyd and quarterd, and their quarteres sette abowte London on every gatte; thes was of them that dyd ryse in the West cuntre.

[a] See the Additional Notes.

[b] "Degovara." (Side note.)

Item the vj. day of Februarij came the duke of Somerset owte of the towere, and lay at the Savoye.

Item the xxx[ti] day of March was Palme sonday, and on the evyne was proclamyd a generalle pes betwene the kynge of Ynglond and the Frenche kynge, and the qwene of Scottes and the realme of the same also, with their subjecttes; and grett bonfyeres with grett chere at every cunstabulles dore in every parich thorrowe alle London; and soo after thorrow alle Ynglonde.

Item the xij[th] day of Aprill, he that was byshoppe of Rochester, Nicolas Rydley, was stallyd [bishop of London] by one of the byshoppe of Ely('s) chaplynes. And the xix. daye of the same monyth he came in to the qwere at the comunyon tyme, and at that tyme he and the dene recevyd and master Barne, and the too toke the host of the prest in their too hondes. And that same tyme the byshoppe commandyd the lytt of the aulter to be put owte or he came in to the qwere.

Item the ij[de] day of May was Jone Bucher otherwyse callyd Jone of Kentte burnyd in Smythfelde for grett herysses, as yt hath bene longe knowyne, and was condemnyd nye a hole yere, as it shewyth before; and there preched before hare or she dyede Scory,[a] and she sayd to hym that he lyed lyke a knave, &c.

Item that Bullyne was gevyn up to the Frenchmen the ij. day of Maij.

Item Nicolas Rydley that was byshoppe of Rochester was made byshoppe of London, and beganne his visitacione in Powlles the v. day of May.

Item that there came a sheppe of egges and shurttes and smockes owte of France to Byllynges gatte.

Item the terme rejurnyd from the Assencion unto Myhylmas.

Item the proclamacion the xxiij. day of May, the wych was the fryday before Whytsonday, was for the pes betwene France and us.

Item on Whytsone sonday preched the byshoppe of London Nicolas Rydley at Powlles crosse.

[a] John Scory, afterwards bishop of Hereford in the reign of Elizabeth.

Item the nyght before came in the Frenche lordes with their tresor &c.

Item on Trenyte sonday preched doctor Kyrkame,[a] and sayd that in the sacrament w[as no] substance but brede and wynne.

Item on sente Barnabes day was kepte [no holi]day (through) alle Londone at the commandment of the mayer, and at nyght was the aulter in Powlles pullyd downe, and as that day the vayelle was hongyd [up] benethe the steppes and the tabulle sett up there; and a sennet after there the comunion was mynysterd.

Item the xiiij. day of June was sattorday, and before evy[ning] was a mane slayne in Powlles church, and ij. frayes with-in the church that [same] tyme afterward.

Item also this yere Corpus Christi was not kepte holy day.

And the Assumpcion of our Lady was soche devision thorrow alle London that some kepte holy day and some none. Almyghty God helpe it whan hys wylle ys! for this was the second yere, and also the same devision was at the fest of the Nativitie of our Lady.

Item the last day of August preched at the crosse Stephin Caston,[b] and there spake agayne the lady Mary asmoch as he myghte, but he namyd not hare, but sayd there was a gret woman with-in the realme that was a gret supporter and mayntayner of popery and superstycione, and prayed that she myght forsake hare oppynyons, and to follow the kynges prosedynges, as he sayed. And also he sayed that kynge Henry the viij^th^ was a papyst, with many obprobryus wordes of hym as yt was harde.

Item this yere was proclamyd that the French crownys shuld goo for vij s.

iiij^o^. A^o^. Thys yere the xiiij. daye of November was proclamyd

[a] Thomas Kyrkham, S.T.P. presented by the Merchant-taylors' company to the rectory of St. Martin Oteswich in London, 8 June, 1548. His successor was instituted by bishop Bonner, by lapse, in Feb. 1554—probably in consequence of Kyrkham having fled the country. Newcourt, Repert. Lond. i. 409, 410.

[b] Stephen Caston, clerk, was presented by Francis Wyatt esquire to the rectory of Sutton in Essex 9 May 1556, and died in 1575. Newcourt, Repert. Lond. ii. 567

thorrow all London that ne wyttelleres nor tabernes shulde kepe no resorte of pepulle in their howses for vyttelles on the sondayes nore holy dayes tyll alle serves ware done, and that shulde be at a xj. the cloke; and also at after-none tylle evynge-songe ware done, in payne of gret prisonment at the kynges commandment.

Item this yere was many frayes in Powlles church, and nothynge sayd on-to them; and one man felle doune in Powlles church and brake hys necke for kecheynge of pegyns in the nyght the iiij. day of December.

Item the v. day of December was proclamyd that the French crownes shuld goo but for vj s. iiij d.

Item at Crystmas was put downe in Powlles the *Rectores chori*, wyth all their coppys at processione, and no more to be usyd.

Item the day of was the byshoppe of Wyssytor[a] comyttyd to the Flett, and the xj. day of December was comyttyd to the Flett the byshoppe of Chechester.[b]

Item the xv. day of December was browte from the tower of London un-to Lambeth the byshoppe of Wynchester thene beynge doctor Stephen Gardner, before the byshoppe of Cauntorbery then beynge Thomas Cranmer, wyth dyvers other comysioneres, and exammynd and comyttyd un-to the tower agayne. And the xviij. day followyng ther agayne; and that same day was too tydes at London brygge within the space of v. howeres, and grett sprynges that dyd moch harme by the watter syde and on the watter. And the sayed byshoppe of Wynchester at Lambyth the viij. day of January [1551], and the xij. day, and so to the towere agayne. The xxvj. day there agayne, and that day browth from the tower unto Lambyth [by the] garde and the offesers of the tower wyth weppens, and soo home agayne; and on the xiij. day of February and xiiij. day also, and that day he was dyschargyd [from] hys byschopryge and alle hys londes, and comyttyd unto the tower agayne.

[a] Nicholas Heath, afterwards archbishop of York in the reign of queen Mary.

[b] George Day, afterwards restored to Chichester by queen Mary.

Item the xxij. day of Marche was Pame sonday, and as that daye [were] put into the Fleete dyvers gentylmen, as sir Antoni Browne, M. *(blank)* sargant of the lawe, wyth dyvers other, for herynge of masse in my lady Mary's curte at sent Jones[a] and was there.

Item the xxiiij. day of the same monyth after was the grattes be-syde the hye alter in Powlles closyd up, that the pepulle shulde not loke in at the tyme of the comunyone tyme, and the vayle hongyd up. And the xxviij. day after was Ester evyne, and then was the tabulle remevyd, and sette benethe at the vayele northe and sowthe; and on Ester day the dene, then beynge Wyllyam Maye, dyd mynys ter hym-selfe.

Item this yere was sene in the Lent besyde Martyn abbe[b] many men in harnes syttynge in the eyere, and soo came downe agayne un-to the grownde and vadyd awaye agayne, and also in dyvers other places. And also abowte Ester was sene in Sussex three sonnes shenynge at one tyme in the eyer, that thei cowde not dysserne wych shulde be the very sonne.

Item the xxv[th] day of May, wych was the monday after Trenyte sonday, was gret ertheqwakes[c] in dyvers places, as abowte Crowy-dyn and in that towne and dyvers other townes there by, as at Rygate, and many other places abowte, and also at Westmyster and dyvers other places in London, and abowte there.

Item in June after went inbassatores into France the erle[d] of Northehamtone and the byshoppe of Ely[e] wyth dyvers other, and was goodly resevyd there with processione, crossys, and sensynge, with alle the holé orders of relygious persons that be there, with the universites, scolles, and solome masse songe before them or they came unto the kynges presens, and had there grett chere. And after that came into Ynglonde dyvers lorddes of France with a cardnalle, and came to Rye the iiij. day of July, and soo unto Lon-don, and was not resevyd. And before their comynge into London

[a] St. John's at Clerkenwell.

[b] Merton priory in Surrey is meant.

[c] See Machyn's Diary, p. 6. [d] *Read* marquess. [e] Thomas Goodrich.

was dyvers lordes and gret men of the ines,[a] and laye at the kynges place in Sothewarke.

Item the ix. day of the same monyth beganne the gret sykenes callyd the swetth,[b] that there dyde a grett multitude of pepull sodenly thorrow alle London and thorrow the most parte of alle Ynglonde. And that same day was the proclamacion for testornes at ix d. And the vitelles as dere after as it was before and worser, that the pepull cryde owte of it in every place thorrow alle the realme.

And the xxvij. day of the same monyth the byshoppe of Wynchester that was than (John Ponet[c]) was devorsyd from hys wyffe in Powlles, the whyche was a bucheres wyff of Nottynggam, and gave hare husbande a sartyne mony a yere dureynge hys lyffe as it was jugydde by the lawe.

Item the last day of July (and) the furst of August rydde in a cartte a tayler of Fletstret and hys syster rydde in a carte abowte London, and bothe ther heddes shavynne, for avouttre, that he had ij. childerne by harre, and the iij[de] day was bannyshyd the citte bothe; but he wolde have gevyne moch to a be scowsyd,[d] but it wold not be tane.

Item the xvij. day of August was a proclamacion at vj. a cloke in the mornynge for the qwyne of testornes of ix d. unto vj d., and grottes unto ij d., and ij d. unto j d., and j d. unto a ob., and ob. unto q.; and it the vitolles [were dearer] than the ware before.[e]

[a] The inns of court. Apparently some eminent legal personages were appointed to wait on the ambassadors.

[b] I have collected some particulars of this epidemic in a note to Machyn's Diary, p. 319. In addition to the two examples there given of its bearing the cant name of *Stop-gallant*, the following entry from the register of Loughborough in Leicestershire may be added: "1551, June. The swat called *New acquaintance*, alias *Stoupe Knave and know thy Master*, began on the 24th of this month."

[c] The name is left blank in the manuscript. This passage is remarkable as a fuller statement of the same matter of which a brief notice occurs in Machyn's Diary, p. 8, and which was only assigned by strong presumption to bishop Ponet. See the note, ibid. p. 320.

[d] excused.

[e] *i. e.* and yet victuals were dearer than they were before.

Item xxiij. day of Auguste the pariche of seynt [Faith ente]rd furst into Jesus chappelle as their parich church and had servys there.[a]

Item the xxvj. of September was the stondynge at the tabulle in Powlles was removyd into the sowth . . . .

Item the viij. day of October was the byshoppe of Chechester[b] and the byshoppe of Worseter[c] conventyd in the byshoppe of London's pallys before the comyssyoners; and the ix. day there . . . and dyschargyd. Theys ware the commyshoners,—the lorde cheffe barne,[d] doctor Olyver, d[octor] Rede, Lyell, Gosnalle, and *(blank)*.

Item un Myhylmas day the kynges grace went in hys robe that was sent hym from the Frenche kynge of the order of sent My[hyl] at Hamtone cortte wyth gret ryalty there at that tyme.[e]

Item the xj. day of October was made, at Hamtone cortte, John Dudley erle of Warwyke duke of Northum[berland, the] markes Dorsett duke of Suffolke, the lord trezerer markes of Wynchester, William Harbart markes of Pembroke.

Item the xvj. day of October was the duke of Somerset, lorde Gray, sir Raffe Vane, wyth many moo (committed to the Tower), as it shall apere after.

Item, the xxj. day of the same monyth beganne the craftes of London to wacche at the gattes of London at vj. in the mornynge unto vj. at nyghte, and continewyd tylle the xxiij. day of November.

vj^{o}. A^{o}. Thys yere at afternone on Alhallone day, whan the mayer came to Powlles, there was dyvers persons of the duke of Northhumberlondes servanttes wolde have tane the chayne from the kynges shreffes necke in Powlles goynge after the mayer, and wolde have made a fraye within Powlles church, but whan they came with-owte the church at the north dore there thei made a fray and fowte and ware departyd, and went in to the pettycannons and

[a] Jesus chapel was in the crypt of St. Paul's cathedral church: see a note to Machyn's Diary, p. 365. The parishioners of St. Faith were placed in this church in 1551: see Stowe's Survay and Newcourt's Repertorium Londinense, vol. i. p. 349.

[b] George Day. [c] Nicholas Heath. [d] Sir Roger Cholmley.

[e] See Machyn's Diary, p. 9, and notes, pp. 321, 397.

fowte there, that whan the mayer came forthe of Powlles church he was fayen to fett them forth and had them to the counter.

Item on the morrow after the qwene of Scottes[a] came in to London by watter, and soo unto the byshopp of London's palles, and lay there; and the morrow after she went unto the corte un-to the kynges grace, and had there gret chere. And the fryday after shee went hare wayes. And dyvers lordes and ladys browte hare on hare way, and whan she came with-owte Byshoppes gatte the fayryst lady that she hade wyth hare of hare cuntre was stolne away from hare,[b] and soo went forth in hare jorné.

Item the viij. day after, the wyche was the tewsday, there was a tayler that dwelte in Aldersgatstret was sett on the pyllery at afternone, and the cause was that whan the mayer went to Westmyster he callyd them alle cokeoldes; and stode there tylle it was iij. a cloke at after-none.

Item at thys tyme was dyvers proclamacions and pricys made for vyttelles, but it servyt not; and the xxviij. of November was made a contrary proclamacyon and sette alle at lyberty agayne, and every viteler to selle as they wolde and had done before.

Item the furst day of day of December was browte the deuke of Somersett owte of the towre by watter at v. a clocke in the mornynge, and j. or ij. drownyd by the waye in the Tems betweene the tower and Westmester; and there he (was) araynyd before the cowncell, and so pletyd for hym selfe that he was qwytt for the treson, and comytted unto the tower of London agayne.

Item the nexte day was the lorde Gray with dyvers other that ware in the tower was browte un-to Westmester un-to the starre chamber, and sent home agayne.

Item the viij. day of that monyth was a gret muster at Totehylle[c] of men of armes befor the kynge, of dyvers lordes.

Item the xvj. day was a proclamacion for the new qwyne[d] that no

[a] See Machyn's Diary, p. 11, and note p. 322.

[b] Whether this fair lady's elopement is elsewhere mentioned I have not ascertained.

[c] In Tothill fields by Westminster. [d] coin.

man [should speak ill o]f it, for because that the pepulle sayd dyvers that ther was the ragyd staffe[a] . . . . it.

Item the xx[ti] day of December was sorne[b] the byshoppe of Ely[c] lorde [chancellor of Engla]nd.

Item that same day was the muster of the dewke of Somersettes servanttes before [the king at] Totylle also.

Item the same day was comytted unto the tower the byshopp [of Dur]hame Cudberte Tunstalle.[d]

Item the xxij. day of the same monyth was be[heddyd] at the Towre hyll before viij. a clocke Edwarde deuke of Somersett [erle of Hert]forde and unkyll unto the kynges grace. And also there was a commandment thorrow London that alle howsolders with their servantes shulde kepe their howses unto it was . . . . .

Item on Crystmas evyn was made a proclamacion that no man shulde make qwoyne, nore send beyond see, in payne of dethe.

Item the iiij[th] day of January [1551-2] the lorde of Crystmas[e] of the kynges howse came thorrow London and thorrow Scheppesyde, and soo to the lorde mayer's to denner, and dyvers of hys corte was devydyd, some to the sherffes and to dyvers aldermen; and agayne after none was made a scaffolde at the crosse in Schepesyde, and thether he came and made hys proclamacion.

Item the xiij. day of January was whyppyd vij. women at the carttes arse, iiij. at one and ij. at another, for vacobondes that wold not labor, but play the unthryftes.

Item the xix. day of Februarij was a man slayne within Powlles churcheyerde.

Item the xxvj. day of the same monyth, the wyche was fryday, was hongyd at Towre hylle sir Myllys Partryge knyght, the wych playd wyth kynge Henry the viii[te] at dysse for the grett belfery

[a] One of the many intimations of the unpopularity of the duke of Northumberland, whose badge was the ragged staff.

[b] sworn. [c] Thomas Goodrich.

[d] —— which had long lain at his house by Colharbor in Thames street. Stowe.

[e] Probably George Ferrars: as in the following year.

that stode in Powlles church-yerde;[a] and sir Raffe Vane, theys too ware hongyd. Also sir Myhyll Stonnappe and sir Thomas Arndelle, theys too ware beheddyd at that same tyme. And theis iiij. knyghttes confessyd that they ware never gylté for soche thynges as was layd unto their charge, and dyde in that same oppinion.

The daye before endyd the parlament.

Item the xvj. day of Aprill was Ester evyn, and that day rydde a woman in a carte abowte London that dwelte in Aldersgate strete that made aqwavyte,[b] for cardynge of hare mayde wyth a payer of carddes soche as doth carde wolle with-alle,[c] and was sende unto warde agayne.

Item wher as it hath of an olde costome that there shulde be three sermons in Ester weke, this yere was a commandment that there shulde be but ij. and that the wedynsday shuld not be kepte holy day.

Item also wher as it hathe bene of ane olde costome that sent Gorge shulde be kepte holy day thorrow alle Englond, the byshoppe of London commandyd that it shulde not be kepte, and no more it was not.

Item lyke-wyse at Wytsontyde was but ij. sermons; they ware lyke-wyse at the crosse, and he that prechyd the sonday prechyd the ij. other, and but ij. dayes kepte holy days.

Item on Wytsone evyne it raynyd in dyvers places in London that it was sene lyynge in dyvers places on the erbbes[d] as redde as wyne.

[a] "Neere unto this schoole (St. Paul's) on the north side thereof, was (of old time) a great and high Clochier or Bell-house, foure-square, builded of stone, and in the same a most strong frame of timber, with foure bells, the greatest that I have heard; these were called Jesus' bells, and belonged to Jesus' Chappell, but I know not by whose gifte. The same had a great spire of timber covered with lead, with the image of Saint Paul on the top, but was pulled down by sir Miles Partridge knight, in the reigne of Henry the Eighth. The common speech was, that hee did set one hundred pounds upon a cast at dice against it, and so wonne the said clochier and bells of the king, and then causing the bells to be broken as they hung, the rest was pulled downe."—Stowe's Survay.

[b] aqua vitæ.

[c] See another account of this cruel mistress in Machyn, p. 17.

[d] herbs, or grass.

Item the iij. day of August betwenne x. and xj. at nyght was a woman in Oxfordshere at a place callyd Midylton-stoné at the syne of the Eggylle viij. myle from Oxforde, and the good man's name was John Kenner, and she was delyveryd of a chyld with too heddes,[a] iiij. hanndes, iiij. fette, and but one body, and the mydwyffe kersende[b] them at home and was alowyd by the churche; and (they) lyffyd xv. days; and ett, and [one slept] wylle the other dyd wake, and lokyd with a mery chere whan anny persons lo[ked at] them. Item also in that same cuntry was a henne hacchyd of a chekyn that had ij. heddes and iiij. fette.

Item in the same monythe was tane at Bl[ack] wall and nere abowte London was tane dyvers dolfyns.

Item the iiij. day of September was apone a sonday, and then the qweer of Powlles had a commandment from the dene from Cambryge at the byshoppe of Cantoberes visitation that he shulde leve the playnge of organs at the devyne servys, and soo lefte it.

Item the iij. day of Octobere was the byshoppe of Dorram than beyng Cudbert Tunstall browte to examinacion at the place that some-tyme w[as] callyd the abbé of Tourehylle, the viij. and the xiij. also that daye he was deposyd of hys see, and commyttyd unto warde agayne.

Item also in this monthe was tane dyvers hother fyches gret in the Temse.

Item the xxv. day of October was the pluckynge downe of alle the alteres and chappelles in alle Powlles churche, with alle the toumes, at the commandment of the byshoppe then beynge Nicolas Rydley, and alle the goodly stoneworke that stode behynde the hye alter, and the place for the prest, dekyne, and subdekyne; and wolde a pullyd downe John a Gauntes tome but there was a commandment [to] the contrary from the counsell, and soo yt was made alle playne as it aperes.

[a] Other descriptions of this prodigy are given by Stowe, and by Machyn, p. 25; and the deaths of the double children ibid. p. 26.

[b] christened.

Item this yere beganne the howse in London for the powre the w[hich] was some tyme the Gray freeres in Newgatte markette, &c.

Item on Alhallon day began the boke of the new servis of bred and wyne in Powlles, with alle London, and the byshoppe[a] dyd the servis hym-selfe, and prechyd in the qwere at the mornynge servis, and dyd it in a rochet and nothynge elles on hym. And the dene[b] with alle the resydew of the prebentes went but in their surples and lefte of their abbet of the universyte; and the byshope prechyd at after-none at Powlles crosse, and stode there tyll it was nere honde v. a cloke, and the mayer nor aldermen came not with-in Powlles church nor the crafftes as they were wonte to doo, for be-cause they were soo wary[c] of hys longe stondynge.

Item the day of thys same monyth[d] the chylderne was put in the howse that was some tyme the Grayfreres.

Item after Allhollanday was no more communyon in no place but on the sondayes.

Item this yere was nether sent Nicolas nor the Concepcion of our Lady kepte holyday, nor it (*sc.* yet) the Assumpcion of our Lady before, nor the Nativite of our Lady; but put downe, &c.

Item on Crystmas day at after-none alle the men chylderne wyth the women chylderne and alle the offesers that perteynyd unto the howse of the powre,[e] stode at the grett condett in Cheppe in a rowe whan the mayer came to Powlles at after-none, and soo home agayne, to be sene of the citte. Item the byshoppe prechyd alle the holydayes in the qwere at evenynge prayer.

Item the iiij. day of January [1553] came the lorde of mysrewle of the corte[f] thorrow London wyth the sheffes[g] lorde, and soo un-to the crosse in Cheppe, and there made a proclamacyon, and so un-to the mayer's to denner, and alle hys corte was devydyd un to dyvers

[a] Nicholas Ridley. [b] William May. [c] weary.

[d] The 23d of November. [e] Christ's hospital.

[f] George Ferrars: see the passage in Machyn's Diary, p. 28, and the note thereupon, p. 328. [g] sheriff's.

aldermen; and amonge alle one parte was commyttyd to master Curtes the alderman, but whan they came thether there was nothynge preparyd for them, for he wolde not be at home, but he was send for, but he wolde not be fownde, wherfor v. of hys servantes ware browte, eche of them had too mene ledde them, unto the mayer's, and soo alle that daye, and soo at nyght unto the corte; and the nexte day they ware sent home. [Item] the mayer dyd gret correccione unto powre pepulle, as rydynge in cartes [and standy]nge on the pyllere, both men and women.

And this yere the furst day of [March was the] parlament, and kepte wythin the kynges pallys at Westmyster, Whythalle.[a]

Item this yere [the town] deche from Newgate unto Aldersgat was stoppyd up with brycke, and made playne [with the er]the.

Item in the begynnyng of May was tane owte of alle the churches of London and abowte [all the] plate and qwyne[b] that was in their boxys in every church for the kynges grace; and vestmenttes and [copes], wyche drew unto a grett substans besyde the coyne, and also this yere was very fewe cherches in London that had anny procession in the Rogacion dayes in London this yere for lacke of devocion.

Item the xvij. day of May the market in Newgate market was removyd unto the new howsys and the shambylles where sent Nicolas church sometyme was, alle save only the mele-men, at the commandment of the mayer.

Item the xxv. day of May satte in Powlles the comyssioners with the lorde cheffe justes, with the lorde mayer, and soo had away alle the platte, coppys, vestmenttes, wyche drewe unto a gret gooddes for the behoffe of the kynges grace.

Item the xxvj. day of May beganne the bishope of Cantorbe(ry) to sytte for the new boke that the byshope of Wenchester, Powny, made, that he wolde have that alle parsons and curattes shulde sette their hondes unto it, and so every byshope in hys dyesses. And in

[a] —— "and the morrowe removed to Westminster." Machyn, p. 32.

[b] coin.

London was dyvers that denyed many of the artycles, as doctor Weston, with dyvers other, as it shalle shoo after.

Item the furst day of June was sett up at the standerde in Cheppe a pyller[a] new made of a good lengthe from the grownde, and too yonge servanddes tayed un-to yt with a chayne that thee myght goo abowte it, and to bettyn with roddes soore on their backes for because they had too wenches in-to their master's howse; and on the morrow after, wyche was the sonday, and then was too other in the same case bettyn at the same pyller, and so as many as plesyd the mayer after-warde, &c.

Item this yere the mayer dyd put in execucion the acte for the hyghth of pentoseese[b] thorrow all London.

Item the ij[de] day of July prechyd doctor Hodskyne[c] that was some tyme suffecane of London, and dyd nether pray for lady Mary's grace nor it *(sc.* yet) for lady Elizabeth; and the nexte sonday after prechyd the byshoppe of London, Nicolas Reddesle, and there callyd bothe the sayd ladys bastarddes, that alle the pepull was sore anoyd with hys worddes, soo uncherytabulle spokyne by hym in soo opyne ane awdiens.

Item the vj. day of July dyde kyng Edward the vj. at Grenewyche, as they say, and some say he was powsynd, as it shalle apere ar-after.

JANA REGINA.

Item the x. day of the same monythe after vij. a clocke at nyght was made a proclamacyon at the crosse in Chepe by iij. harraldes and one trompet with the kynges shreffe of London master Garrard

[a] See constant instances of the use of this pillar in Machyn's Diary ; and on one occasion (p. 109) it is called "the post of reformation." From the obscure orthography both of that and this chronicler it is liable sometimes to be confounded with the pillory—an instrument of punishment apparently of the same original etymology.

[b] Penthouses: noticed also by Machyn, p. 35.

[c] John Hodgeskynne, suffragan bishop of Bedford: see Newcourt, Repertorium Londinense, i. 153.

with dyvers of the garde for Jane the duke of Suffolkes dowter to be the qwene of Ynglond, (but fewe or none sayd "Good save hare,"[a]) the whyche was browte that same afternone from Richemond un-to Westmyster, and soo unto the tower of London by watter. And the nexte day in the morninge was sett forth in printe that the lady Mary with the lady Elzabeth ware bothe provyd illegittimatt and borne unlawfulle and clerely dyschargyd from the crowne and from almaner of possessions of the kynge their fader Henry the viij. And also provyd accordynge by the lawys of the churche, as thei say, and by the temporall lawys. And also by a parlament kepte at Westmyster in the xxviij^{ti} yere of their fader kynge Henry the viij. And soo by that they be dyschargyd and dyssanullyd from alle maner of inherrytans of the imperialle crowne of the hole realme of Ynglond, and to have none maner of possessyons of the same. And they say also that the kynge Edward the vj. made a wylle and a testament at hys last dayes, and gave the inherytans of the crowne unto the duches of Suffolke lady Kateryne, the whiche was dowter un-to lady Mary that was the Frenche qwene and one of the dowters of kynge Henry the vij. and yf she had anny male issew or the sayd kynge Edward the vj. dyde, then the imperiall crowne shulde goo unto here issew, and if not un-to here dowter lady Jane the wych was maryd unto the iij. sone of the duke of Northhumberlond Gylford Dudley. And from hare for lacke of issew unto hare cosyne Margaret late the dowter of lady Elnor wyffe unto [the earl of Cumber]lond one of the kynges blode, the whyche was one of the French qwens dowters [and to the heirs] of hare body lawfully begottyne.

. . . . a yong man that was drauer at sent Jones at Ludgate . . . . both hys erres cut of cruelly, and sent unto warde agayne . . . . and had a rewarde of the chamber;[b] and within iij. dayes after hys

[a] These words are a subsequent insertion above the line.

[b] This paragraph (which is very imperfect from being written in the upper margin of the manuscript, where it is partly burnt and cut away,) relates to the story of Gilbert

master [went to the Tower, where he was] gunner, and was drownyd by the way and ij. men with hym.

Item the xij. of the same monyth of July was [procl]amacyon made to take up men, and to come to Totylle, and to have xd. a day, and .na[mely to] feche in lady Mary; and that same day wente furth to feche here in the duke of Northhumberlond, and more was se . . . . . but he lay a iiij. or v. dayes besyde Ware, and then went forwarde to Chambri[dge, and] thowte to worke masteres,[a] as it aperes after.

MARIA REGINA.

Item the xix. day of the same monyth, [which] was sent Margarettes evyne, at iiij. of clocke at after-none was proclamyd lady Ma[ry to] be qwene of Ynglond at the crose in Cheppe with the erle of Shrewsbery, the erle [of Arundel], the erle of Pembroke, with the mayer of London, and dyvers other lordes, and many of the ald[dermen] and the kynges schrffe master Garrard, with dyvers haroldes and trompettes. And from thens cam to Powlles alle, and there the qwere sange *Te Deum* with the organs goynge, with the belles ryngynge, the most parte alle [London], and that same nyght had the [most] parte of London *Te Deum*, with bone-fyers in every strete in London, with good chere at every bone[fyer], the belles ryngynge in every parych cherch, and for the most parte alle nyght tyll the nexte daye to none.[b]

Item the xxij. day of the same monyth was tane the duke of Northhumberland at Cambryche by the mayer, and proclamyd a traytor, and soo kepte in a prysone tyll they harde from hare grace and hare cownselle. And on saynt James day at after-none at iiij. of cloke at after-none was browte unto London worshyppfully as he had deservyd, and browte in at Byshoppes gatte by the erle of Arndelle,

Potter, of which the particulars have been collected in the Chronicle of Queen Jane and Queen Mary, pp. 115—121. The present passage states, that on the change of affairs he received an immediate "reward of the chamber" of the city, and it has been shown in the former chronicle that he had afterwards a more ample recompence from the crown.

[a] masteries. [b] noon.

the wyche browte hym unto the tower of London. And whan he came in at Byshoppes gate he was commandyd to put of hys atte, and soo dyd tylle he came to the tower; and after he came onsse to Shordych alle the pepulle revyled hym and callyd hym traytor and herytycke, and woulde not seyse for alle the(y) ware spokyn unto for it. Wyth hys sones, as the erle of Warwyke, Ambrose Dudley, Henry Dudley, Androw Dudley,[a] the erle of Huntyngtone, lorde Hastynges, sir John Gattes that was captayne of the garde, and sir Henry Gattes hys brother, sir Thomas Palmer, doctor Saunder. Item here went the byshoppe of London[b] that was goynge un-to the qwene to begge hys pardon, but he was tane at Ipsege, and there was put in warde.

Item the xxij. day of the same monyth began the wache at every gatte in London in harnes, viij. be syde the viij. comeners.

Item xxvj. day of the same monyth was browte to the tower of London at ij. a clocke at after-none doctor Redley that was the byshope of London, lorde markes of Northhantone, Roberte Dudley that was the dukes brother,[c] master Corbet that was shreffe of Essex, and after them that same nyght was browte in sir Roger Chamle[d] cheffe justes of the kynges bench, sir Edwarde Montageu cheffe justys of the comyn place; and the next day came in sir John Jorke[e] and Sir Thomas Wrathe,[f] with dyvers other, as it shalle apere afterwarde.

Item the iij. of August came in the qwenes grace[g] after vij. a clocke at nyght from Newhalle with the lady Elzabeth hare syster, and a grette company of ladys wyth hare; and she goodly imparelde with alle the resydew of hare ladys, and so to Whytte-chappell; and there the mayer with the aldermen reseved hare, and he delyveryd hare the swerde, and she toke it to the erle of Arnedelle, and he bare it before hare, and the mayer the masse.[h] And whan she came at

[a] Sir Andrew Dudley, K.G. was his brother.
[b] Nicholas Ridley.
[c] Lord Robert Dudley, afterwards earl of Leicester, was the duke's second son.
[d] Cholmley.
[e] Yorke.
[f] Wroth.
[g] Compare with Machyn, p. 38.
[h] mace.

Algate there it was goodly hangyd with clothes, banners, and stremers, and syngers, and goodly aparelde alle the way downe to Ledynhalle, and hangyd with clothes, banners, and stremers, and syngers, as is above sayd; and also on the one syde the crafftes of London with-in raylles in their best aparelles and clothe hangynge before theme; and so downe Graschesstret and in-to Fanchersse strete, and soo downe Marke lane, and soo to the towere; and every hows hangyd as is above sayd, wyth syngers, organs, and shalmes; and whan she came to the tower, that she was with-in the tower, ther was soche a pelle of gonnes what bothe smalle and gret and soo longe and soo thecke that hath not be harde; soo gladde dyd the pepulles harttes rejoyse in hare comynge in, as God save hare grace, and longe to contynew, and prosper hare in goodnes! Amen.

[The v.] of August at vij. a clocke at nyght came home Edmond Boner byshoppe [from the Ma]rchelse lyke a byshoppe,[a] that alle the pepulle by the way badde hym welcom home [both] man and woman, and as many of the women as myghte kyssyd him, and soo came to Powlles, and k[nelt on the] steppes and sayd hys prayeres; and then the pepulle range the belles for joye; and whan he left the Mareshelsey there came in doctor Cokkys[b] for hym. And the nexte day the duke of Norfoke, the byshoppe of Wynchester,[c] the byshoppe of Durrham,[d] the byshoppe of Chechester,[e] and the byshoppe of Wyssiter[f] had their pardone, and ware dyschargyd, and soo went abrode and restoryd un-to there [dig]nytes agayne alle hole.

Item the vj. day of August was lefte the wache at the gattes in London.

Item the vij. day of the same monyth was the kynge Edwarde the vi. removyd un-to Whythall un-to Westmyster by the byshoppe of Canntorbery wyth-owte any crose or lyght; and berryd the nexte

[a] See Machyn, p. 39.

[b] Richard Cox dean of Westminster, afterwards bishop of Ely in the reign of Elizabeth.

[c] Stephen Gardiner. [d] Cuthbert Tunstall. [e] George Day.

[f] Nicholas Heath.

day with a comynyone and that powely,[a] and the byshoppe of Chechester[b] prechyd a good sermon.

Item the xiij. day of August prechyd master Borne[c] at Powlles crosse at the commandment of the quenes grace, and there was pullyd owte of the pulpyt by vacabonddes, and one threw hys dagger at hym.

Item the xviij. day of August was the duke of Northumberlond[d] was browte by watter un-to Westmyster with the markes of Northhamtone and the yerle of Warwyke hys sone, and there was condemnyd by them-selffes and had no qwest went apone them but them selfe, and submyttyd them selfe un-to the qwenes grace and here lawys; and the nexte day both the Gattes and Andrew Dudly the duke's brother and Palmer in lyke wyse condemnyd.

Item the xx^ti day of August prechyd at Powlles crosse master Watsone,[e] and there was dyvers of the quenes cownselle, and the captayne of the garde with a CC. and more of the garde browte hym to the pulpytte, and stode there alle the sermone tyme with ther halberttes.

Item the xxij^ti day of the same monyth sufferd at Tower-hyll the duke of Northhumberlond, sir John Gattes captayne of the garde before, and sir Thomas Palmer, alle three beheddyd; and the day before harde masse in the tower and reseved the sacrament in forme of brede.

Item the xxix. day of August satte the qwenes commissioneres for the new byshoppes, that was put in for them that was put owte and in to prisone at the commandment of the byshoppe of Cauntorbery as is above sayd, and as it shalle follow.

[a] Poorly. A note referring to the accounts preserved of this ceremonial will be found appended to Machyn's Diary, p. 331.

[b] John Scory.

[c] Gilbert Bourne, soon after bishop of Bath and Wells: see the present incident also in Machyn, p. 41, and the note from the chronicles and privy council register, ibid. p. 332.

[d] See the Chronicle of Queen Jane and Queen Mary, pp. 16, 121.

[e] Thomas Watson, soon after bishop of Lincoln: of this sermon see also Machyn's Diary, p. 41, and William Dalby's letter, ibid. p. 332.

Item in August was the aulter in Powlles set up agayne, and fenysyd[a] in September.

Item the xiiij. day of September was the byshoppe of Cauntorbery comyttyd unto the tower from the sterrechamber, Thomas Creme[b] by hys name; and the xv. day was comytted also unto the tower the byshopp of Bath [William] Barlowe by name.

Item the same tyme was alle the new byshoppes dyschargyd and put downe.

Item the xvij. day of September the byshoppe of London, Boner, sangc masse in Powlles, and gave holy watter hym-selfe, and soe continuyd.

Item the laste day of September was the qwenes grace browth from the tower of London unto the Whyth-hall goodly, and many pagenttes in dyvers places as she came by the wey in London, with alle the crafttes and aldermen, and also a pagent in Powlles churcheyerde at the est ende of the church, and there she stode longe, for yt was made of rosemary with alle here armes and a crowne in the myddes. Item also there was a man made too tope-castelles above the crosse of the stepulle, and there stode with a flagge in hys honde and viij. flagges hangynge besyde; and a castelle made in the myddes of the hye waye at the denes place. And the furst day of October she was crowned at Westmyster by the byshoppe of Wynchester Stephyn Gardner, and she was browth from Westmyster halle with iij. crosses with a gret qweer and many byshoppes with their myteres on their heddes and crose-stavys in ther honddes, as many as had none other lette, and they had other that bare them before them; for as that tyme she wolde not suffer non to be in the qweer nor to mynyster in hare presence, that in soomoch she had alle that was in Powlles save only them that ware maryd, that in somoch that the day was no servys in Powlles, nother mattens nor masse nor evynsonge [nor] sermone at the crosse as that day.

Item the vth day of the same monyth beganne the parlament; and

[a] finished. [b] Cranmer.

whan they ware in the parlament howse the byshoppe of Lyngcolle doctor [John Taylor[a]] beynge byshoppe of Lyngcolne hys parlament robe was tane from hym and he was comy[tted] to the tower; and iij. dayes in the weke the qwene satte in the parlament howse and harde alle soche thinges as was there done.

Item the vij. day of October beganne the convocacion in Powlles, aud there had [mass of] the Holy Gost. And there the byshoppe of London sange the mass in hys *pontyficalibus*, and that [was the] furst masse that was songe at the hye alter after that it was sett up agayne, and had a good[ly] sermon *ad clerum* in the qwere.

Item the xxj. day of that same monythe beganne the dyspu[tacion] in the longe chappell in Powlles betwene the new sortte and the olde, as monday, wedyns[day, and] fryday, and there came moche pepulle; but they ware never the wyser, and with many worddes of . . . . , that the qwenes graces cowncell was fayen to send worde that there shulde be no more dy[spu]tacions, but that it shulde be dyscussyd by the hole parlament. And as at that tyme the wet[hercock] of Powlles stepulle was tane downe, and new made and gyltyd, and sett up agayne the iiij. day of November.

Thys yere the xiij. day of November the byshoppe of Cantorbery Thomas Creme[b] and lady Jane that wolde a bene qwene, and iij. of the Dudleyes[c] condemnyd at the yelde-halle for hye tresone.

Item this yere the qwere of Powlles went abowte the stepulle on sent Kateryns day at nyght.[d]

Item on sent Andrewys day begane the generalle procession in Latten in Powlles churche,[e] with the parsons and curattes of London, with the prebenttes in their gray ammes, and the mayer with dyvers of the aldermen; and the same wyse iij. dayes followynge.

Item the vj. day of Januarij [1554] came from the emperor im-

[a] He and John Harley bishop of Hereford had withdrawn from the solemnization of the queen's coronation at the commencement of the mass. He died soon after at Ankerwick. (Foxe).

[b] Cranmer.

[c] Lord Ambrose, lord Harry, and lord Guilford. See Chron. of Q. Jane, &c. p. 32.

[d] See Machyn, p. 49.

[e] Vide ibid.

bassotors in the name of the hole howse of Bowrgone, as dyvers erles, as the erle of Degmonde[a] with dyvers other.

Item the xiiij. day of Januarij began the procession on the sondayes abowte the church[b] with the mayer and the aldermen in their clokes, and the precher takynge hys benediccion in the body of the church of the bysshoppe.

Item the xv. day of the same monyth began the insurreccion at Maydstone by sir Thomas Wyett knyght, lorde Cobhame,[c] Harper, and Colpeper, with dyvers others.

Item the xvj. day of the same monyth in the mornynge began the wache at every gatte in London in harnes, both men and their servantts, etc.

Item the furst day of Februarij the qwenes grace came (in) hare owne persone un-to the yelde-halle of Londone, and showyd hare mynde[d] un-to the mayer, aldermen, and the hole crafttes of London (in) are owne persone, with hare cepter in hare honde in tokyn of love and pes, and wente home agayne by watter at the Crane in the ventre.

Item the xxiij. of Januarij was condemnyd at the yelde-halle of London lorde Robert Dudley.

Item the xxx[ti] day of the same monyth the duke of Norfoke came to Strode, and bent hys artyllery agaynst Wyett; but the Londoneres with their captayns, as Brian, Fyztwilliams, and Bret, whoo came with the duke agaynst Wyet, made a shoute and fled from the duke to Wyet, that the duke hardly scapyd from them.

Item the furst day of Februarij came Wyett with hys host in to Sothwarke at iiij. a clocke at after-none, and or it was v. he had made a bulwarke at the bryge fotte, and kepte Sothwarke tyll it was

[a] Egmont, see the note to Machyn's Diary, p. 337. See also the Chronicle of Queen Jane and Queen Mary, p. 34.

[b] St. Paul's.

[c] Lord Cobham was at first suspected of taking part in Wyatt's rebellion: see the Chronicle of Queen Jane and Queen Mary, p. 36.

[d] Her address to the citizens is given by Foxe.

the vj. of the same monythe, and dyd no harme there; and this was Shroft tewsday; for the brygge drawebrygge was drawne agayne hym, and the nyght before many of hys men fled from hym; and the same tewsday was ij. men hongyd on a gybyt in Powlles church-yerd be-fore sent Gregory's. And that same day Wyet with hys host departyd owte of Sothwarke at ix. a cloke in the mornynge, and went un-to Kyngstone. And also at that same tyme the duke of Soffolke with hys brother was tane by the erle of Huntyngtone; and that same day was *Te Deum* songe in the qwenes chapelle for joye of it. And that same day the lorde Cobhame[a] and Harper whar put in-to the tower. [The vij.] day Wyet with hys host came un-to the parke besyde sent James and soo wolde [have entered, and there] most traytorys shott at the corte gattes that the arres stoke there longe after. And he hymselfe came in at Te[mple bar, and] soo downe alle Fletstrete, and soo un-to the Belle savage. And then was hys trayne [attacked at] the comandment of the erle of Pembroke, and sartayne of hys men slayne. And whan [he saw] that Ludgatte was shutt agayne hym he departyd, saynge "I have kepte towche," and soo went [back] agayne; and by the Tempulle barre he was tane, and soo browght by watter[b] unto the [tower] of London. And then alle the qwens host came thorrow London goodly in araye with sperys. And that same day was tane one William Albryght parsone of Kyngstone besyde Barrame downe,[c] precher of the gosspelle, besyde Charynge crosse in this rebellyone. Also it is to be supposed that Wyett hadde come in at Ludgat had not one John Harres a merchant-taylor in Watlynge stret [ha]d not sayd, "I know that theys be Wyettes ancienttes;" but some were

[a] Lord Cobham, though he had not joined the rebels, was compromised by the conduct of his sons. He was released with his son sir William on the 24th of March 1553-4: see Chronicle of Queen Jane and Queen Mary, p. 71, and Machyn's Diary, p. 58. His son Thomas was condemned, but afterwards pardoned. (Bayley's Tower of London, p. 445.)

[b] He was carried first on horseback to Whitehall. See the Chronicle of Queen Jane and Queen Mary, p. 50.

[c] Kingston, co. Kent, five miles from Canterbury.

very anggre wyth hym because he sayd soo, but at hys worddes the gattes ware shutte.

Item the viij. day of Februarij the ducke of Suffolke wyth hys brother was browte thorrow Londone wyth a goodly company of spere-men, and soo unto the tower of London.

Item the xij. of Februarij was beheddyd wythin the tower lady Jane that wolde a bene qwene; and hare husband whose name was Gylford Dudley at the Tower-hyll.

Item the xiiij. day of the same monyth for the same rebellyon was hongyd one Vicars a yeman of the garde, Bouthe one of the quenes fotmen, gret John Nortone, and one Kynge; and in severalle places abowte London at the gattes, in Cheppe syde, and other strettes, to the number of xx[ti], the wych ware of London that fled from the duke of Norfoke; and that same day was iij. hongyd in chanys on Hay hylle for the same offence in rebellyon.

Item the duke of Suffolke was condemnyd at Westmyster the xvij. day of Februarij; and beheddyd at Towre-hyll the xxiij. day of the same monyth.

Item the xv. day of March was commytted un-to the tower agayne the erle of Devenchere.

And the xviij. day of the same monyth was commyttyd also unto the tower lady Elzabeth that was the quenes syster, and that was Palme sonday.

Item the epestylle masse begane agayne[a] the ij. day of Aprille.

Item the viij. day of Aprille was a katte hongyd on the gallos[b] in Cheppe clothed lyke a preste, and that same day hylde up before the precher at Polles crosse.

And shortly after the qwenes grace gave a generall pardon for alle thoys that ware with Wyet, and som(mon)ed a parlament to be helde at Oxforde, but it was sone rejurnid unto London agayne unto Westmyster.

[a] In St. Paul's cathedral.

[b] This is also noticed by Foxe, Stowe, and Machyn: see Machyn's Diary, pp. 58, 338.

Item the xj. day of the same monyth was Wyett behedyd at Towre hylle, and also qwarterd; and hys hedde with one of hys qwarteres sett apon the gallowys, and the hed with the qwarter was stolne awaye.

Item the ix. day of Aprille began the opposycions at Oxford by Thomas Creme [a] sometyme byshoppe of Cantorbery, Nicolas Rydley sometyme byshoppe of London, and Hugh Latemer, agayne the lerdemen [b] of both the universytes; and there the sayd iij. persons was condempnyd as erytykes, and soo remaynyd there in presone a longe tyme.

Item the xxvij. of Aprille was beheddyd at Towre hylle the duke of Suffolkes brother.[c]

Item the xiiij. day of May was the monday in Wytsone weke and thene the mayer, aldermen, goldsmythes and fyshemongeres [d] came a procession un-to Powlles as they were wonte to doo, but there was no sensynge; and dyvers other pariches came alle the iij. dayes as they ware wonte.

Item the xviij. day of May was draune from the tower of London Thomas a Vane [e] unto Tyborne, and there put to execucion.

Item the xxiiij. day of May was Corpus Christi day that some kepte holy day and some wolde not, and there was a joyner that dwelte in Colmanstrett, hys name was John Strett, he was in Smythfelde whan the procession of sent Pulchers came by hym, and he wold a tane the sacrament from the prest,[f] but he was resysted and tane and put in Newgatte, and then he faynyd him-selfe madde.

[a] Cranmer. [b] learned men.

[c] Lord Thomas Grey: see Machyn, p. 61, and Queen Jane and Queen Mary, p. 75.

[d] This was in revival of an ancient custom by which the companies of the Goldsmiths and Fishmongers were associated on certain festivals. See a paper by the Editor of the present volume in the Archæologia, vol. XXX. "On an amity formed between the Companies of Fishmongers and Goldsmiths of London, and a consequent participation of their Coat Armour."

[e] This is a mistake: the sufferer on that day was William Thomas, late clerk of the council: see Machyn, p. 63, and the Chron. of Queen Jane and Queen Mary, p. 76.

[f] See also Machyn, p. 64; and Foxe.

Item the iiij. day of June was tane downe alle the gallos within London.

Item the x. daye of June was sonday and thene was a goonne shotte nere Powlles cherch-yerd that the pellyt came nere the precher's face that preched at Powlles crosse.[a]

Item the xxij. day of June was a proclamacion made for shottynge wyth hand-gonnes and berynge of weppons.

Item the furst day of July was . . . . and whereas there was in the parich of sent Gregory's one John Hyllc a cutler [that was] obstenatt that wolde not beleve in the blyssyd sacrament of the alter, nor it (*sc.* yet) tylle the[n ha]d not resevyd it; but he was conventyd be-fore hys ordenary the dene of Powlles [that] was at that tyme doctor Facname,[b] and soo revokyd hys opynyone opynly before all the pariche, and askyd them mercy and foryefnes for his evylle insampulle, and prayd them to pray for hym, and then and there he resevyd the sacrament opynly befor them alle.

Item the . . day of the same monyth, wher as ther was a mayd that spake in a walle[c] in a howse [in] Aldersgat stret stode at the Powlles crosse before the precher doctor Wymbsle[d] archedekon of [Middlesex], and there shoyd alle the hole matter and asked God mercy and the quene, and alle the pepulle, for ar evy[ll] insampulle. And the xviij. day of the same monyth stode a man on the pyllery for the same matter, with a paper and a scryptor on hys hed, that was consentynge there-to.

Item the x[ix] day of the same monyth the prince of Spayne came in at Hamtone, and there was goodly resevyd.[e] And the

[a] Compare with Machyn, p. 65.

[b] John Feckenham.

[c] Of this imposture see Machyn's Diary, pp. 66, 339; and Tytler, ii. 340.

[d] John Wymmesley, or Wymunsley, one of the natural sons of George Savage, priest, and consequently a natural brother of bishop Bonner. He was archdeacon of London from Oct. 1543 to April 1554, and then archdeacon of Middlesex until his death in Oct. 1556. See Newcourt, Repert. Londinense, i. pp. 63, 81, 211.

[e] Full particulars of the reception and marriage of king Philip will be found in the Chronicle of Queen Jane and Queen Mary.

xxij[ti] day of the same monyth, the wych was Mary Maudlyne day, at nyght was commandment gevyn in London to have bonfyers and belles ryngynge thorrow alle Londone. And the nexte day to have *Te Deum* in every church for joye of hym. Item the xxiij. day of the same monyth he came to Wynchester, be-twene vj. and vij. at nyght, where he was honorably and goodly resevyd. And the xxv. day of the same monyth was honorably marryd with gret solemnite with many honorabull lordys and ladys, and men of worchypp as it dothe apere, both spiritualle and temporalle. Item the furst day of August was a proclamacion made in London for the hole stylle[a] bothe for the kynge and the qwene and alle ther domynyons of both. They came not unto London tyll it was the xviij. day of Aulgust, and then came bothe unto the place in Sothwarke, and lay there that nyght. And the xix. day came into London, wher they ware goodly resevyd with many pagenttes, as furst at the brige fotte, and alle the howses on the brigge new payntyd whyt and yellow, and in Grachhed strett a goodly pagent and costly; and another in Cornelle; and one at the Gret Condet, and at the standerd the wayttes of London playnge; and the crosse in Cheppe new gyltyd and that costly, and the gènologe of hym at the Lyttyll Condet; and alle the crafftes of London stondynge be the way in their best aparelle in alle the strettes as he came goodly hangyd, and soo to Powlles; and there was goodly resevyd of the byshopp wyth the prebenders and the holi[b] qweer of Powlles, and soo into the qwere, and there was *Te Deum* songe. And there was one came downe from the chapter-howse apon a roppe. And soo departyd un-to Westmyster. And Ludgatte new payntyd. And a pagent in Fletstret at the cundet. And so un-to the pallys of Whythalle. Item on sent Luke's day the kynge came un-to Powlles, and ther harde masse, and went home agayne.

[a] Their whole royal style. See Machyn's Diary, pp. 34, 67, and the Chronicle of Queen Jane and Queen Mary, p. 142.

[b] *So the MS. but no doubt for* whole.

Thys yer the iiij. day of November prechyd at Powlles crosse doctor (Harpsfield)[a], and there was v. men, as iij. prestes and ij. temporalle men, dyd opyn pennans. The iij. prestes ware maryd. One was a challon of Esynge spettylle,[b] and one a blacke frere, and the iij. an Austyne freer. And this was their pennans: furst to come owte of the vestre with shettes apone ther backes, and eche of them a rodde in their honddes wyth a taper lych,[c] and furst came and knelyd before the hye aulter, and there the suffrecane gave them their dyssipline; and than went downe before the crosse: and whan the precher had tane hys benediccion of the byshoppe in the myddes of the church, they came downe unto the byshoppe, and knelyd downe in the myddes of the church, and there had their dyssiplines of hym, and he kyssyd them; and soo went unto the crosse, and stode there alle the [sermon] tyme, and whan he came unto the beddes[d] they turnyd unto the precher and knelyd downe [and asked forgive]ness there of hym, and then he showyd their oppynyons opynly in the pulpyt.

Item the xij. day [of November] began the parlament at Westmyster, wher as the kynge rode in hys parlament robe, and [the que]ne in an opyne charret by hym,[e] on the ryght honde of hym, goodly aparelde and rychely [in a robe of cri]msone velvyt and cloth of golde; with alle the lorddes in their parlament robbys bothe spiritualle [and tempor]alle. And there was [a serm]on, in the whych was the pope prayd for at the masse of the Holy Gost.

And the nexte day came the convocacion at Powlles, and the masse of the Holy Gost there also, and a sermon in the qwere *ad clerum*, and there the pope was prayd for also by name.

Item the xix. day of November began the pluckynge downe of the postys at the corte gatte at Westmyster by the hyeway syde for the play of the Spanyardes that was callyd the cane.[f]

[a] John Harpsfield, archdeacon of London: see Machyn, pp. 73, 340.

[b] A canon of Elsing spital.

[c] lighted.

[d] The prayers.

[e] Compare with Machyn, p. 74.

[f] The juego de cannas: see Machyn's Diary, pp. 76, 82, 83; and note in p. 389.

Item the xxiiij. of the same monyth came in the cardnalle Powle by watter, and soo came unto the corte at Whythalle; and in the myddes of the brygge the kynge mette hym, and soo eche other salute other goodly and reverently; and soo wente in unto the qwene, and soo she mett them at hare gret chamber, and she salutyd hym; and there they talkyd a whylle, and he departyd un-to the place at Lambyth the wyche was preparyd for hym.

Item the xxv. day of the same monyth was sent Kateryns day, and that day was the play at the corte gatte of the cane: in the wych the kynge with alle the lordes and soch as plesyd hym came from Dyrraham place[a] goodly aparelde unto the place, and there playd, and havyng their targattes on their sholderes; and thankys be to God that there was no harme done there.

Item the xxviij. day of the same monyth was a sermon in the qwere of Powlles, and *Te Deum* songe, with a generall procession[b]; and the byshoppe in hys myter and dyvers other byshoppes in their abbettes; the mayer [and] aldermene in their scarlett with their clokys, and alle the crafttes in their best aparelle; and the nexte day was procession in every parich in Londone with *Te Deum*.

Item that same day at afternone came the cardnalle un-to the corte, and shoyd hys mynde unto the kynge and qwene and the councelle, with dyvers of the parlament howse, and soo departyd to Lambyth agayne.

Item the ij. day of December after was the furst sonday of Advent, and that day the sayd cardnalle came unto Powlles, and there was reseved of the byshoppe of London and the byshoppe of Wynchester, then beynge chaunsler of Yngland, at the church dore, and alle the parich churches of the dioses of London, parsons, vicars, and curattes, in their coppys, with their clarkes holdynge their crosses with their banneres.

Item the xvij. of the same monyth came in the prince of [Piedmont[c]] at after-none by watter, and soo to the cortte.

[a] Durham place in the Strand.

[b] In thanksgiving for "the queen's quickening:" see notes to Machyn, p. 341.

[c] See Machyn, pp. 79, 341. Emanuel Philibert prince of Piedmont, and duke of Savoy,

Item the vth day of Januarij [1555] was sent Edwardes day and thene was sett up the scrynne[a] at Westmyster, and the aulter, with dyvers juelles that the qwene sent thether.

Item the xxv. day of the same monyth was the Conversione of sent Paulles day, and then was a generall procession[b] with the chelderne of alle the scolles in London, with alle the clarkes, curattes, and parsons, and vikeres, in coppes, with their crossis; and the qwere of Powlles in lyke wysse; and dyvers byshoppes in their habbettes, and the byshoppe of Londone in hys pontificalles and coppe, berynge the sacrament under a canyppy, and iiij. prebenttes berynge it in ther gray amos; and soo up unto Ledynhalle with the mayer [and] aldermen in scarlet, with their clokes, and alle the crafttes in their best aray; and soo came downe agayne on the other syde and soo to Powlles agayne; and then the kynge with my lorde cardnalle came to Powlles and harde masse, and went home agayne; and at nyght was commandment gevyn to make bonfiers thorrow alle Londone for joy of the pepulle that ware convertyd lyke wyse as sent Powlle was convertyd.

Item the iiij. day of Februarij was John Rogers, that was sometyme viker of sent Sepulkeres and reder in Powlles and prebendary after doctor Royston,[c] burnyd in Smythfelde for gret herysy. And Hopper and [*blank*] send un-to Glociter, and ther to (be) burnyd lyke wyse; [and di]vers more un-to other places.[d]

had been the first person elected into the order of the garter in the reign of queen Mary. He was cousin-german to king Philip by their mothers, and it was contemplated that he should marry the princess Elizabeth. See Tytler's Edward VI. and Mary, ii. 448 *et seq.*

[a] The shrine of saint Edward: but it had not been fully "set up again" at the beginning of the year 1557: see the passage in Machyn's Diary, p. 131.

[b] Compare with Machyn, p. 80.

[c] John Rogers was instituted to the prebend of Pancras, vacant by the death of John Royston, D.D. on the 24th Aug. 1551. (Newcourt, Repert. Lond. i. 196.) He was appointed reader of the lecture in St. Paul's by the dean and chapter: and is fully commemorated by Foxe as the protomartyr of the Marian persecution.

[d] At the same time that bishop Hooper was sent to Gloucester, Lawrence Saunders was sent to Coventry, and Rowland Taylor to Hadley: see Machyn, p. 82.

Item on Ester day was a prest at sent Margaryttes at [Westminster bro]kyn on the hedde and on the arme wyth a wood knyffe in minysterynge of the blyssyd [sacrament] un-to the pepulle in the church. And soo he [a] was tane and sent unto the tower of [London], and the thursday after was browte unto Newgate; and the fryday browte un-to Pow[lles, and] saterday after also, and there was desgradyd of the byshoppe of London in the con[sis]tery, for he was . . . . . and a prest before. And there in the presens of the cheffe justys of the comyne place, the lorde m[ayer], and the shryffes, and soo commyttyd unto Newgatt agayne; and the xxiiij. day carryd unto W[estminster] and there burnyd for that same dede.

Item the xxv. day of March was another generalle process[ion], and then was delyveryd a poddynge unto one of the prebendes goyng in procession. Item the same man the xxvij. day of that same monyth was betten with whyppes at the peller in Chepe at the standert.

Item the vij. day of Aprelle the Observanttes ware put in at Grenwych agayne by the bysshopp of Rochester, Morys,[b] that was some tyme a blacke freere, at the commandment of the quene.

Item the xxix. day of May another generalle procession unto sent Maggolles [c] and soo downe Temstret, and up at Dougat and soo to Powlles.

Item the xxx[ti] day Cardmaker [d] with another with hym burnyd in Smythfelde for heryse.

Item the xxxj. day of the same monyth was a proclamacion for the blyssyd sacrament and for bokes of scypter.[e]

[a] *i. e.* the man who committed the assault. He had been a monk of Ely: see Machyn's account of the same occurrence, p. 84, and also Strype, Memorials, iii. 212.

[b] Maurice Griffin, consecrated bishop of Rochester April 1, 1554.

[c] Saint Magnus, which was by popular corruption called Saint Magnol's.

[d] John Cardmaker, late vicar of St. Bride's, before mentioned in p. 56. His fellow-sufferer was John Warne, upholster of London: see a full relation in Foxe.

[e] Scripture. I have not been able to trace a proclamation of that date; but on the 14th of the next month (see Machyn, p. 90) was issued a proclamation for the suppression of heretical books, including the Book of Common Prayer, which is printed at length by Foxe.

Item the xxvij. of June was kept the obijt of the kynges grandhame,[a] with a goodly herse as ever was sene, and stode a vj. or vij. days after.

Item the xxvj. day of August the kynge and the qwene came thorrow the citte, and soo to Grenwyche towarde in hys jurné unto hys fader the emperar; and there toke hys leffe.

Item the xvj. day of October was burnyd at Oxforde doctor Ridley that was sometyme byshoppe of London, and doctor Lattimer, for gret herysy.

Item the xxvij. day of September after was the counter in Bredstret removyd in-to Wood-strete.

Thys yere was dyvers burnyd in many places in Ynglond. And the xxvij. day of Januarij [1556] was burnyd in Smythefelde v. men and too women for gret heryse.

Item the iiij. day of November began the parlament at Westmyster. And the xj. day after began the cardnalles senod at Lambyth, and contynewyd tylle the xij. day of February after.

Item the mayer with the citté enterde into Brydwelle.[b]

Item the xxiij. of February was Shroft sonday, and then was leppe yere, and that day the byshoppe of London Edmonde Boner, the byshoppe of Lyncolne then beynge [John White], and the byshoppe of Ely doctor Thyrlebe, satte at Oxforde in commyssoners for the pope aponne Thomas Creme[c] some tyme archebyshoppe of Cantorbery apone hys gret heryse that he was in, and there he was desgradyd of hys leggatsheppe and of hys archebyshoppecheppe, and presthed, wyth alle other ecclesiasticall degres, and presthode, and soo comyttyd unto the temperalle honddes and jurysdycion.

Item the xxj. day of Marche followynge was burnyd there and

[a] The king's grand-dame here mentioned was Jane queen of Spain, the heiress of Castile and Arragon: and who was also queen Mary's maternal aunt. See Machyn's account of the hearse and the ceremonial, which took place in St. Paul's cathedral church, at p. 90 of his Diary, and the note thereon, p. 344.

[b] They then took possession of that royal palace: whose name has subsequently become the generic term for houses of penal discipline throughout the country.

[c] Cranmer.

thether was send by the cownselle the lord John Wyllyams with dyvers others to see the execucion done.

Item the xxviij. day of the same monyth was Newgatte a fyer; but, thangkes be to God, that there was but lyttyll harme done, for it was sone qwenched.

[The . . .] day of May was *(blank)* ware hongyd, draune and qwarterd . . . .

Item the xviij. day of the same monyth was captayne Taunton drawne from the tow[er to Tybo]rne, and there hongyd and qwarterd.

Item this tyme was dyvers burnyd in Smythfelde [for he]rysy.

Item the viij. day of June was draune from the tower of London unto Tyborne [Throg]mortone, Wooddalle, Stantone, Bedelle, Rosselle, and Darrelle, ware hongyd, hedyd, [and] qwarterd for robery and tresone.[a]

Item the viij. day of June was hongyd at Towre-hylle master [Pec]kams sone and Danyell for gret robery.[b]

Item the x. day of the same monyth was a yonge man hongyd within Brydewelle for robery within the sayd howse.

Item in the same monyth [be]gane the procession in every church, that the chylderne with their parentes shuld goo monday, wedysday, fryday, and sondayes with their bokes in their hondes or beddes[c] every person, and one of a howse, on payne of forfettynge of xij d. at every tyme. And the churchwardens with other too that be shsyne[d] by the hole paryche; and yf that they doo not loke substancially apon it that then they to forfett ij. s. and the sayd mony to be bestoyd on the church at the discrecion of the sayd commyssinores; but it was but lyttyll lokyd apone, and the more pytté.

Item the xviij. day of August the mayer[e] dynned at the rederes[f] denner at the Tempulle, and at after-none whane he was goynge the

[a] See Machyn's Diary, pp. 102, 105, and notes, pp. 348, 349.

[b] See Machyn, pp. 109, 351.

[c] beads.

[d] chosen.

[e] Sir John Lyons.

[f] The reader.

swerde was willed to be borne doune in the closter, [but the sword-berer woold not[a]].

Item in this same monyth was many herytykes browte owte of Essexe, and owte of other places.

Item the vth day of September was browte thorrow Cheppesyde teyd in ropes xxiiij[ti] tayd to-getheres as herrytykes, and soo unto the Lowlers tower.[b]

[a] These words were inserted above the line, and subsequently scratched through with the pen: at the same time the words "torne from hym" were altered to "willed to be borne doune."

[b] At St. Paul's: see note to Machyn's Diary, p. 346.

ADDITIONAL NOTES.

P. 1, l. 7. The word imperfect in the MS. is in Arnold's Chronicle, "Portchaf," *i. e.* Port Jaffa or Joppa.

P. 15, l. 4. For "Stawe" *read* Strawe.

P. 22. *A blacke sterre.* So our MS., but in Arnold's Chronicle "a blasing starre," *i. e.* a comet.

P. 26, 4th l. from foot. "*And this yere was brent a palmer.*" This is a flagrant clerical error of the MS. In Arnold's Chronicle we read "this year was brent ye towne of Paburh'm." Qu. was this Baburham or Babraham, co. Cambridge?

P. 30. *Evil May-day and John Meautys.* In the fuller account which Stowe gives of these riots, he relates that the mob ran from Cornhill "to a house east from Leadenhall, called the Green Gate, where dwelt one Mewtas, a Pickard or Frenchman, within whose house dwelled divers Frenchmen, whom they likewise spoiled, and if they had found Mewtas they would have stricken off his head." The present chronicle tells us how he escaped,—by hiding in the gutters of his house. The history of that house, "a fair house of old time called the Green Gate," will be found in Stowe's Survay, where he states that "John Mutas, a Pickarde or Frenchman, dwelt there, and harboured in his house many Frenchmen that kalendred wolstedes, and did other things contrary to the franchises of the citizens." This John Meutas, or Meautys, (called James in the present chronicle,) founded a family in England, of which a pedigree will be found in Clutterbuck's History of Hertfordshire, vol. i. p. 93, and some further account in the memoir accompanying the portrait of Sir Thomas Meautys, (sometime secretary to lord chancellor Bacon,) engraved for the Granger Society.

P. 31. *Alice lady Hungerford.* The passage relating to this execution is extracted by Stowe from the present chronicle, which is cited in his margin as the "Register of the Gray Fryars," but he has inserted after the lady's name the following words,—"a knight's wife, for murthering her husband." In order to recover some further particulars of this domestic tragedy, I applied to the Rev. J. E. Jackson, of Leigh Delamere, Wilts, who has made large collections relative to the family of Hungerford, and he obligingly favoured me with a reply, which, with the view of exciting further inquiry, was inserted in the Gentleman's Magazine for December 1851. The question is stated thus :—

It appears that Sir Richard C. Hoare, in his volume on the Hungerfords (Hungerfordiana, p. 20) has introduced the name of Alice lady Hungerford and her catastrophe as belonging to the wife of a Robert Hungerford of "Cadenham." This appropriation is most improbable, for these reasons :—

1. None of the Cadenham Hungerfords were of the rank of knight before a Sir George, who died in 1712.

2. In the Hungerford pedigree printed by Gough, the name of Alice, as a wife, does not appear at all in that branch of the family.

3. Supposing Sir R. C. Hoare to have had some authority which he has not produced for assigning the wife Alice and the story of the murder to the Robert Hungerford of Cadenham to whom he has assigned them, still his account is contradicted by dates. According to him that part of the Cadenham pedigree would stand thus :—

Robert Hungerford (grandfather).=Margaret Long.

Robert Hungerford (father).=. . . . .

Robert Hungerford (grandson, =Alice.
the presumed murdered man).

Now, Robert the grandfather died in 1558 (see his will abstracted in Collectanea Topog. et Geneal. vii. 71); Robert the father was buried at Bremhill in 1596; so that Robert the grandson, if murdered in 1523, must have been murdered 35 years before the death of his grandfather, and 73 years before that of his father. In the absence, therefore, of all reference to authority, Sir R. C. Hoare's statement must be regarded as a mere guess.

Mr. Jackson then proceeds to state that he has, in his own mind, long fixed this story upon other parties in the Hungerford family; but that, in his turn, he can produce no authority for it, except that of a little circumstantial evidence.

At the date of the execution, A.D. 1523, the existing knights of the Hungerford family were these—

1. Sir Walter Hungerford of Farleigh Castle, the then head of the family, who was created Baron Hungerford of Heytesbury in 1536.

2. Sir John Hungerford of Down Ampney.

3. Sir Anthony Hungerford, also of Down Ampney, his son.

Now neither of the two latter persons could be the knight alluded to; for Sir John died between 24 July and 27 August 1524 (see his will, Coll. Top. et. Gen. vii. 71), leaving his wife *Margaret* surviving him; and Sir Anthony lived to 1558, was buried at Great Bedwyn in that year, and his wives' names were *Jane* (Darell) and *Dorothy* (Danvers).

Sir Walter Hungerford of Farleigh Castle (afterwards Lord Hungerford of Heytesbury) is the only person in the entire Hungerford history upon whom the least probability of connexion with the story can be attached. To him there is this great objection *in limine*, that he was certainly not murdered by his wife in 1523, because he was beheaded in 1541. But it will be observed that our Chronicle merely records the fact of the lady's execution, and that the crime for which she is stated to have suffered was inserted by Stowe from some other authority. Stowe relied, perhaps, on traditional information, which may easily have varied in some degree from the truth It is probable that the lady may have been tried and condemned on a charge of *attempt to murder*, instead of having actually caused death. With this variation of the fact as stated by Stowe being granted, there are circumstances in the domestic life of this Sir Walter Hungerford which lead to the conclusion that the story refers to him.

In the first place, as we have seen, he was a knight at the time, and moreover the only one in the family then existing to whom it can refer.

In the next place, he was married three times: 1st, to Susanna Danvers; 2dly, to *Alice*, daughter of the Lord Sandes; and 3rdly, to Elizabeth (or Isabella), daughter of Lord Hussey. The date of the first wife's death has not been ascertained, but he was certainly married to the third wife before the year 1532. So far, circumstances favour Mr. Jackson's conclusion.

In a very curious letter, written about the year 1536, to Cromwell Lord Privy Seal, Elizabeth Hussey, the third wife, applies for justice and protection against her husband, on account of his cruelty. He had charged her, most falsely as she declares, with incontinence; had arbitrarily shut her up and kept her close prisoner for four years in one of the towers of his castle, without money, and with only such food as was brought to her by a chaplain, a creature of his, who, she says, "had undertaken to get rid of her out of his lord's way." That she was afraid to eat what this person brought her, and was secretly supplied by the poor women of the village at the window. She goes on to say "that she could tell, if she dared, many detestable and urgent crimes on the part of her husband, as he well knew," and especially of his notorious cruel conduct "always to his wives."

With this letter to illustrate the character of Walter lord Hungerford, considering also that names and dates are all consistent, it may at all events be admitted as a fair suggestion that the lady executed at Tybourn may have been the second wife, Alice Sandys; that his cruelty to her may have driven her to attempt to get rid of him by poison, or that he, wishing to get rid of her (as he did afterwards of his third wife), may have brought some accusation against her, and procured her condemnation. Such things were done in those days. Above all, when the reader is referred to p. 42, and is apprised of the crime for which this wretched man at last suffered the extreme penalty of the laws there is so much reason to conclude he had long outraged, it will not be thought unjust that the stigma should at length, in the pages of history, be removed from one of his victims to himself.

P. 31, l. 14. For "master George Monop," *read* Monoux. A large MS. volume of vellum, filled with transcripts of deeds and other documents relating to the estates of Sir George Monoux, was sold in the auction room of Messrs. Puttick and Simpson, Dec. 4, 1851, Lot 163, for 5*l.* 10*s.*, and has since taken its place among the Addit. MSS. of the British Museum.

Ibid. l. 22. Erase the comma after "January;" and in line 23 for "Ally" *read* Allyn (see p. 33).

P. 35. *Poisoning of the household of the bishop of Rochester, and the punishment by Boiling.* This crime occasioned great popular excitement at the time, which was probably increased both by the supposition that the life of the bishop (John Fisher) had been attempted, and by the rumour that many of the poor which had partaken of his alms had died, which is directly asserted as the fact by Stowe. Such, however, was not actually the case: only one of the episcopal household, and one poor widow, lost their lives. As the parliament was sitting, the matter was brought before it, and an act (22 Hen. VIII. c. 9) was passed, reciting that "now in the tyme of this presente parliament, that is to saye, in the xviij^th^ daye of Februarye in the xxij. yere of his moste victorious reygn, one Richard Roose late of Rouchester in the countie of Kent, coke, otherwyse called Richard Coke, of his moste wyked and dampnable dysposicyon dyd caste a certyne venym or poyson into a vessell replenysshed with yeste or barme stondyng in the kechyn of the Reverende Father in God John Bysshopp of Rochester at his place in Lamebyth Marsshe, wyth whych yeste or barme and other thynges convenyent porrage or gruell was forthwyth made for his famylye there beyng, wherby nat only the nombre of xvij. persons of his said famylie whych dyd eate of that porrage were mortally enfected and poysoned, and one of them, that is to say, Benett Curwen gentylman therof is deceassed, but also certeyne pore people which resorted to the sayde Bysshops place and were there charytably fedde wyth the remayne of the saide porrage and other vytayles, were in lyke wyse infected, and one pore woman of them, that is to saye, Alyce Tryppytt wydowe, is also thereof now deceassed: our sayde Sovereign Lorde the Kynge, of hys blessed disposicion inwardly abhorryng all such abhomynable offences because that in maner no persone can lyve in suertye out of daunger of death by that meane yf practyse therof should not be exchued, hath ordeyned and enacted by auctorytie of thys presente parlyament that the sayde poysonyng be adjudged and demed as high treason. And that the sayde Richard for the sayd murder and poysonynge of the said two persones as is aforesayde by auctoritie of this presente parlyament shall stande and be attaynted of highe treason: And by cause that detestable offence nowe newly practysed and comytted requyreth condygne punysshemente for the same; It is ordeyned and enacted by auctoritie of this present parlyament that the said Richard Roose shalbe therfore boyled to deathe withoute havynge any advauntage of his clargie. And that from hensforth every wylfull murder of any persone or persones by any whatsoever persone or persones herafter to be comytted and done by meane or waye of poysonyng shalbe reputed, demed, and juged in the lawe to be highe treason; And that all and every persone or persones which hereafter shalbe lawfully indyted, appeled and attaynted or condemned of such treson for any maner poysonyng shall not be admytted to the benefyte of hys or theyre clargye, but shalbe immedyatly committed to execucion of deth by boylynge for the same."

It has been supposed that this was an *ex-post facto* enactment, so far as Richard Roose was concerned; and yet we find by the present chronicle, p. 30, that, at an earlier period of Henry's reign, nine years before, a man was sodden in a cauldron at Smithfield, "because he would have poisoned divers persons." Therefore the same punishment appears to have previously attached to the offence. It has not, however, been traced to still earlier times. (See "Notes and Queries," 1852, vol. v. pp. 32, 112, 184.) A third instance of its execution has been found in the chronicle of King's Lynn, about the same time as Roose's case: "1531. This year here was a maid boiled to death in the Market-place for poisoning her mistress." (Ibid. p. .) A fourth occurs in 1542, which is briefly mentioned in p. 45 of the present volume, and somewhat differently by Stowe, as follows: "The 17 March [*i. e.* a week later] Margaret Davy, a maid, was boiled in Smithfield for poisoning of the household that she had dwelled in." Sir Walter Scott, in his Border Minstrelsy (notes to Leyden's ballad of Lord Soulis), gives this passage with the erroneous date of 1524, following a misprint in Stowe's margin. The punishment by boiling is supposed to have been repealed by the statute 1 Edward VI. c. 12, by which all *new* treasons were abolished.

P. 65. *Peter college, next the dean's place in Paul's church-yard.* Stowe, in his Survay, does not tell us what Peter college was, but he thus mentions the accident recorded in the text, somewhat differently as to the particulars: "Then is the Stationers' hall on the same side [south-west of the cathedral church], lately built for them in the place of Peter college, where, in the year 1549, the 4th of January, five men were slain by the fall of earth upon them, digging for a well." I am inclined to think that "Peter College" was a perverted name of the Petty-canons' college, of the foundation of which in 17 Ric. II. Stowe gives some account in a previous passage.

P. 72. *The fairest lady that she had of her country was stolen away from her (Mary of Guise dowager queen of Scots).* It has been kindly suggested to me, (Notes and Queries, v. 305,) in answer to an inquiry on this passage, that the lady in question was probably the same lady who is mentioned in the following passage of a letter of sir John Mason, the English ambassador in France, to the privy council, dated the 18th April, 1551: "The Scotish queen's shipping is hasted very much. It is thought she shall embark a month sooner than she intended. The lady Fleming departed hence, with child by this king [Henri II.] and *it is thought that, immediately upon the arrival of the dowager in Scotland, she will come again to fetch another.* If she so do, here is like to be a combat, the heart-burning being already very great; the old worn pelf [Diana of Poictiers, then aged fifty-three,] fearing thereby to lose some part of her credit, who presently reigneth alone, and without empeasche." And again, from Amboise, April 29, "The said post hath brought word, that the lady Fleming is brought to bed of a man-child, whereat our women do not much rejoyce." Mr. Tytler (History of Scotland, 1842, 8vo. vol. vi. pp. 374, 375) states his suspicion that this lady was Jean, widow of Malcolm third lord Fleming, herself a natural daughter of James the Fourth of Scotland, by Agnes Stewart, countess of Bothwell, or by her sister lady Isabel Stewart, who were the natural children of James earl of Buchan, natural brother of king James II. (Douglas's Peerage of Scotland, by Wood, i. 52, 227, 268). Were this the frail lady Fleming of the year 1551, it might have been said that she was but following the bad examples of her forebears: but as she was married in 1524-5, and had two sons and four daughters, and two of the latter became widows in 1547, their husbands being then killed together with lord Fleming himself (in his 53d year), at the battle of Pinkie, it is pretty clear that Mr. Tytler was mistaken. It is to be feared that the lady Fleming was not a widow, but the *wife*, of James fourth lord Fleming, who was employed as one of the representatives of the Scotish nation to negociate the marriage of their queen, and who died at Paris on the 15th Dec. 1558, æt. 24. She was the lady Barbara Hamilton, eldest daughter of James duke of Chatelherault (at this time regent of Scotland); whose only child named in the family pedigree is Jane (afterwards the wife successively of lord chancellor Thirlestane and of John fifth earl of Cassilis,) who, as she died in 1609, æt. 55, was born in or about 1554. (Wood's Douglas, i. 332; ii. 634.)

P. 94. *The shrine of Edward the Confessor.* This and the other royal monuments in Westminster abbey have recently engaged an unusual degree of attention in consequence of the proposals made for their restoration. It has been remarked that a memento of the re-erection of the shrine in the reign of Mary—a work which, as shown in the note already given in p. 94, occupied some time,—still exists in a monogram of the initials of abbat Feckenham (I F A *i. e.* Johannes Feckenham Abbas) at the end of the inscription on the cornice. Originally there was a different inscription (see Dart, ii. 23, Neale and Brayley, vol. ii. p. 69), part of which has been recently seen, from the plaster having fallen away. It may be presumed that the wooden superstructure of the shrine, the classical architecture of which has puzzled many critics, was a portion of the work renewed by abbat Feckenham.

INDEX.

The reader is apprised that this Index is partial, and confined principally to such matters as might not be readily found by means of the chronological arrangement of the text. To events of familiar notoriety, and the actors in them, particularly those in the earlier and more summary portions of the Chronicle, it will be easy to refer without the intervention of an Index.